JUST MORE OF THE BERKSHIRE FARMER

The Author and his dog

Just more of the

BERKSHIRE FARMER

by Bert Houghton

ISBN 0 9514193 1 5

Front cover illustration by Jane Whitaker.

Produced through MRM Associates Ltd.
322 Oxford Road, Reading, Berks RG3 1AD

Typesetting by TCT Fullpoint London SE1

CONTENTS

Foreword

Following on from my first published book, 'Not just a Berkshire Farmer', I have been asked so many times if there is to be a sequel, The popularity and success of my first amateur attempt as an author has never ceased to amaze me. That readers of all age groups from both town and country seemed to have found something in the pages that gave them pleasure, humour or nostalgic memories has given me encouragement to dig into my memory and diaries for another 'dose of the same medicine'. I trust the reader will excuse my occasional lapse into the Berkshire dialect.

The pleasure of walking or driving through beautiful countryside, enjoying the ever changing colours of the fields, hedgerows and trees can be a just reward for one who makes his living by being a farmer.

Our family at Mousefield have farmed and tended the countryside to the north of Newbury for seventy years, any neglect would be deemed a sin, not for money nor wages, just our duty to the soil and to those who will come after.

This book is dedicated to all those who have made it possible.

August 1991

ACKNOWLEDGMENTS

I would like to express my thanks to those who have helped me and I am indebted to:

My step-daughter Mrs Sue Bourne for editing the original manuscript and the Introduction;

Valerie King for typing the manuscript;

Jane Whitaker, Artist/Designer for the Illustrations;

Edward Mant, Artist, age 12 years;

Mr Andrew Perris for the cover photographs;

Mr Roger Chapman for valuable information on the Newbury Show and finally, to my wife Ruth, for her continuous encouragement and help in the many hours of painstaking research.

Free Land

The dawn of the twentieth century found my father's parents farming at Boxford which is near Newbury in the Royal County of Berkshire. They lived in Westbrook Old Manor long known as Knapp's Farmhouse which is reputed to be 17th century. The Knapps, wherever they may have made their home are to be found in the Church Records as far back as 1629 when an entry quoted earlier says, "William married Elizabeth Knapp". The bride seems to be of far greater importance than the poor groom! Both my Grandparents died before I was born. 'Grandma' Houghton died and was laid to rest in Boxford Churchyard 8.6.1918 aged 67 years. My Grandfather, James Mander Houghton passed away less than a year later 26.4.1919 in his seventieth year.

They had been blessed with five children, James Ralph, Hilda Kate, Douglas Wilfred, Frank (my father) and Delcie Winifred. With some of the older members already married, the small estate of two hundred acres could not support all the family. With this fact in mind in 1908 the whole household made the momentous decision to emigrate. Years later my father was to return once more to farm in England, marry a yeoman's pretty daughter and raise a family. Fired with the spirit of youth, full of ambition, he travelled to Canada on a shoestring budget only to return with little more than his shirt, plus a host of stories in which he had experienced hope, happiness, misfortune, untold hardships and many reckless adventures. In those golden years of childhood, long before the distraction of the 'Box' I liked nothing better than to sit by the log fire on winter evenings enthralled to hear my father repeat again and again tales that probably had lost nothing in the telling. Free Land - several million square miles of virgin prairie in the Canadian West, there for the taking by any adventurer who wanted it. This offer precipitated one of the greatest migrations in history. When vast territories were purchased by the Canadian Government from the Hudson Bay Company in 1869 for 300,000 pounds it was just a wilderness inhabited by a few thousand nomadic Indians, settlements of Buffalo Hunters and a handful of Fur Traders. In 1896 the Dominion Government passed the "Homestead Act". For the sum of ten dollars (two pounds in those days) an adult male could become the proud owner of a quarter section (160 acres) of farm land, plus, for another ten dollars an option on an adjoining quarter. He agreed to erect a shelter, live on his property for the minimum of six years at the same time "break" at least fifteen acres of ground each year. Then the land was his.

What a heaven sent opportunity this offer meant to the land hungry peasants of Europe. They came in droves, crossed oceans, rode trains and walked the prairies. They came too for the right to live their own lives in their own way and in freedom, something they hadn't always had.

The economic prosperity of Canada depended on these sod farmers as producers of grain. Europe was papered with posters, pamphlets and advertisements promising free land in the golden west, an enchanted paradise, invigorating climate, the best wheat land in the world, the richest grazing and unlimited wealth. In reality life on the prairie was one of great privation, a constant battle against the elements with winter temperatures often 40 degrees below zero. Drought, heat, dust storms and mosquitoes plagued the short summers. Crops wiped out by hailstorms, tornadoes or early frosts.

If there was unlimited wealth my ancestors never found it. Dad grew corn, selling oats at harvest time for 5 cents (one shilling) a bushel. Some farmers found prices so low they plowed round the crop and set light to it, it just didn't pay to harvest.

In retrospect my ancestors failed in their quest for financial wealth, but they gained immeasurably in other ways, Their indomitable pioneering spirit still rubs off on our family today - almost one hundred years later.

But I digress: let us start at the beginning: the family left home in mid-March. It was to be four months or more before they arrived at their final destination. Days, weeks, months had been spent packing, settling affairs, selling off stock, paying outstanding bills and saying last farewells to old friends. They had purchased one-way tickets planning never to return to the land of their birth. Few of the family had ever travelled more than twenty miles from Boxford, still to this day a beautiful unspoilt village nestling on the edge of the Berkshire Downs.

The long train journey north to Liverpool which had to be made before crossing the Atlantic was an adventure in itself!!

Right from the start things went wrong. The ship was three days late arriving at Liverpool having been delayed by severe gales en route. The family joined other would-be immigrants, sleeping in a doss-house surrounded by their belongings with little to eat and time on their hands.

My father told me that for months he had dreamt of the luxury liner that was to transport them thousands of miles across the calm, blue waters of the north Atlantic Ocean. In reality the ship turned out to be a filthy, grey, rat-infested ex-troop ship that had returned from the South African War. Equipped to carry eight hundred passengers, by the time it left dock, overloaded with freight and passenger's chattels, there was over 2,000 souls crammed on board. The shipping company was in business to make money, this was no pleasure cruise. As for the Atlantic, it must surely be one of the maddest, wildest places on this planet!

The passengers occupied different parts of the ship. First class in the upper cabins, second class one deck down. The Houghton contingent travelled steerage, billeted in the stern in what had once been cattle decks. These passengers were restricted to their own section, other parts of the ship were out of bounds. Rows of bunks in tiers, each with a life preserver, mattress and a blanket left just enough room to walk inbetween. Down the centre of an adjoining large room was a long, rough boarded oak table where meals were taken. My father described the meals as mysterious yet interesting, often the source of some amusement sitting down with others guessing what some of the dishes were composed of. It was often all too evident, when someone found half a sausage amongst the potatoes and greens, that yesterday's left-overs from the first class restaurant were never wasted!

Two main meals were served each day, just enough to keep body and soul together. At 8 pm cheese and ship's biscuits were issued. These biscuits were six inches in diameter, one inch thick and hard as cement. Dad took his ration to his bunk to chew away at leisure!

The crossing took three weeks, they ran into one great storm after another, tremendous seas tossed the ancient craft around like a cork in a river in flood. Many passengers who had never previously seen the sea, let alone sailed on it, were desperately ill. My father told me that he had never prayed so much in all his life, he was quite positive he would never see land again.

My late Aunt was sea-sick on the whole journey and vowed she would never set foot on another boat. A vow she and uncle Ralph kept. They never returned to England with the result that I now have more cousins in Canada than on this side of the ocean. (Thirty seven at the last count.)

On the twentieth day, to the great relief of everyone on board, land was sighted. The southern rocky coastline of Newfoundland was to starboard as they steamed through the Cabot Strait into the Gulf of St Lawrence. They cruised on for days travelling hundreds of miles up the great waterway now free of winter ice, finally docking south of Quebec City. The immense relief all shared to step once more onto dry land after such an epic ocean crossing can well be imagined, a few passengers had died on the journey, two had committed suicide and one was lost overboard.

I quote extracts from a letter sent home to confirm their safe arrival.

Unfortunately undated.

"Dear Uncle James,

I am sorry that we have kept you such a long time without news, but we have had to be very busy, but am hoping to be still more busy. Well first I must tell you, we had an awful time on the boat, very poor food, in fact I could not eat it at all, and the accommodation was fit only for cattle. I could never have believed anything could be so bad, we were all mighty glad to see land I can tell you, I have not been right since. I happened to take some butter with me, so I had bread (and bad stuff too) and my own butter, it was almost all I did have excepting food which came from the 2nd class waiters at famine price. We could also buy apples on the boat at 3d each. We find apartments very dear out here, we are paying $4,00 for just one room, bed sitting room combined per week. We have to buy all our food out, or else I think the living might be a little cheaper here if anything, but of course it costs like sin to have all meals in a restaurant, and not so nice either, I think you would hardly know me if you saw me now, for I look most unsightly. Both G.G. and I have got a rash come out all over us, but my face, it is simply awful, and I cannot leave them alone, G.G. has got them on his eyes and one of his eyes is very badly swollen, poor kid he does look funny. He says he is going to write you a long letter when the has a little more time to spare. Please give our love to all at Boxford."

The railway had been laid, running north of the great lakes as far as Winnipeg passing through the provinces of Quebec and Ontario, a land of rocks, trees and water, but it was to be almost a week before my father and the family could get tickets.

At last the colonist train arrived, The locomotives and carriages, much larger than those back in England. Two enormous engines pulled the long line of coaches and one more pushed behind, each had a big bell which was rung at every road or rail junction. A large headlight illuminated the track at night and on the front engine was a cow-catcher-cum-snowplow.

The train was crammed full of immigrants. Would-be homesteaders from a dozen European countries. Dad spoke of Germans, Turks, Hungarians, Dutchmen, Austrians, Russians, Ukrainians, Estonians, Lithuanians, even Icelanders as well as religious groups such as Doukhobors, Mennonites and Hutterites.

Stopping at every station progress was painfully slow, often no more than ten or fifteen miles per hour. Even today the line across the prairie is single track with passing places which means long waits for the priority freight travelling in the opposite direction. Coaches were not heated and there was no food unless you took your own. Every coach had a stove at one end with a cistern of water so that passengers could warm some soup or make tea. Our little group made up beds on the floor like the rest of the passengers.

Sleep came only from sheer exhaustion, as the train crept ever westwards. On the first part of the journey they were disappointed not to see rich farmland, for days and nights they travelled across the rocky terrain of the precambrian shield, which covers more than half of Canada's land surface. There were still remnants of ice and snow on higher ground for winter lingers long in that vast country. On the third day the calm radiance of the afternoon vanished, it became dark as night, minutes later the blizzard struck. Father said, "Looking out of the windows we couldn't see five yards, it was a mad, mad world of ferocious winds and driven snow".

Progress became even slower. The drivers stopped the engines, reversed to charge forward at the packed snow, eventually even this failed and they spent the night being buried deeper in the snowdrifts. The fire in the stove had gone out, it was bitterly cold, enthusiasm for this wonderful country was dying fast. Early morning all the men were given shovels, proceeding to dig the train free, but the task was hopeless, the snow blew back again as fast as it was cleared. One week after setting out from Quebec they pulled into Winnipeg Station - the end of the line. The iron horse went no further. The settlers would have to walk the rest of the way. The trek west had now begun in earnest!!

I was given to understand that our little party of would-be sod breakers spent ten days in Winnipeg. It was in this frontier city that they purchased all that was required to set themselves up on their new land. Between the whole group they had just over 5,000 dollars having exchanged their pounds at the rate of 5 dollars to the pound. This had to purchase all their requirements and keep them in food until payment came in for their first harvest some eighteen months ahead. With so many colonists in town prices were high, there were plenty of resident Canadians out to make a fast buck.

The province of Saskatchewan with its slightly rolling terrain offered the nearest unclaimed land. They made the decision to head for Saskatoon 600 miles west!

Young, fit, well broken horses were required for this sort of travel across the roadless, windswept prairie but prices were exorbitant. My father and Uncle Doug were the chief negotiators but they were up against local traders who saw those green Englishmen coming. Four horses, long past their prime, eight oxen, two mules, an in-calf cow and two pigs completed their livestock purchase. They had no intention of breeding from the pigs, they would be killed off in the autumn and salted down for winter. Two covered wagons and a box cart were loaded to capacity with plows, harrows, seed corn, tools, ropes, skinning knives and much more. The food wagon contained flour, sugar, salt, coffee, cooking oil, a plentiful supply of drinking water, and wooden kegs of "high wine" - a patent mixture of rum, brandy and sherry. With rifles and an ample supply of ammunition, fresh meat could be obtained on the trail. My father took pride in the fact that he was a crack shot, with plenty of jack rabbits, prairie

"Westwards, ever westwards towards the setting sun"

chicken and ducks around they were unlikely to starve on the two months journey.

El Dorado - the promised land beckoned, but the year was passing, there was no time to lose. Their goal at the end of the rainbow was a bare, flat, windswept section of virgin land. Some sort of shelter for man and beasts had to be constructed before the terrible Canadian winter set in. If they died from exposure no-one would mourn their passing in this wild, untamed land.

The slow moving oxen set the pace. The only time they moved fast was if thirsty. Dad said, "Those darn beasts could smell water two miles away, and if they took it into their heads, nothing on earth could stop them no matter what was hitched behind their asses!" Two of the ladies in the party were pregnant which must have been the cause of some misgivings. My late cousin Harry Houghton was born on the trail thus becoming the first of our family to be a true Canadian. My first cousins, Phil Povey and the late Basil Povey were both born in Saskatchewan.

They slept in tents or under the stars, woke at dawn, watered the stock, let them graze on prairie grass for a while. They then brewed a billy-can of black coffee, cooked some beans, attended to nature, rounded up the hobbled horses, hitched them to the wagons, moved on again, resting up through the heat of the day in the shelter of a dried up slough. Plodding on in the cool of the evening, westward, ever westwards following the setting sun. No trail, no roads, no trees but occasionally a small settlement where a group of homesteaders had put down roots which gave some encouragement and a chance to renew essential supplies.

They made for North Battleford, now a beautiful city straddling the banks of the North Saskatchewan River, but in those days little more than a village. Dad and his brothers, travel weary, dusty, unshaven and unwashed made for the Dominion Land Office only to be confronted by the rear end of a huge queue of other would-be applicants of the "Land Rush". They waited patiently all day only to be told, "Come back tomorrow, you guys, don't panic we shan't run out of land in a hundred years".

Rising extra early next morning they made sure they were in the front this time. They held their position with difficulty, a group of unsavoury characters made it quite clear that it was not going to be first come, first served if they had their way. I understand the scuffle was brief but not unblooded!!

For the prescribed ten dollars (£2) my father got his quarter section. 160 acres of bald-headed, virgin prairie situated west of the third meridian, in the Rural Municipality of Grass Lake, Number 381, Reward, Saskatchewan. The other men in our family group got the same amount - all adjoining, laid out in sections each of one square mile. All they had to do was mark out their claim, drive a wooden peg in at each corner, live on the ground, work it for six years, at the end of that time, if they survived, they became the proud owners. Yet still their journey wasn't over, leaving North Battleford they now headed south-west making for the tiny settlement of Unity. Although they possessed a rough map and a compass they missed it, going too far south, which added two days to their travels. When they did arrive they rested up for three days, staying at the only saloon in town. Dad paid 5 cents for his first hot bath in three months?

Good advice was given by the bar-tender, "You folks going homesteading then"? "Sure thing, thats why we've come halfway round the world for" they replied.

"Well, first thing you gotta do is build yourselves a shelter, a Canadian winter is mean, man, real mean. Forty degrees below, you'll freeze to death in no time at all if caught in the open. Just fall asleep and not wake up. We get snow blizzards out here, last for days and you can't see your hand in front of you, not even your own feet, and another thing, don't forget put a rope from yer door to the privy or you will never find your way back again in a blow. Happened before you know."

Reaching their future homestead at last dad said, "It was not a bit like I had expected. It was so desolate, not a sign of any other human habitation, not a road or track leading anywhere, nothing but coarse prairie grass blowing in the wind as far as the eye could see in every direction". They pitched tents, hobbled the oxen, tethered the horses and set up a cooking stove out in the open. After a few days they split up onto their respective adjoining sections. Dad, the only batchelor mucked in with his brother Douglas and sister-in-law, my late Aunt Gussie. First they built a shelter for the livestock and dug a well for water.

No trees grow on the alluvial plains of Saskatchewan, a limited amount of firewood and fence posts can be cut from brushwood which grows in the shelter of sloughs. Straight spruce poles to support the house roof, for doorways and such like could only be obtained by going north to the tree line. Dad and Uncle Doug volunteered to undertake this essential task. Setting off with four horses, riding one each with two in tow. Hand saws. axe, ropes and provisions, which consisted mainly of pemmican, (dried and pounded meat). Going north they followed the Hudson Bay trail until it veered north-east through Manitoba. My father often repeated the tale of how they laid up for two days in an Indian camp on the reservation, they were well treated, plied with food, even offered the warm company of a squaw at night until he started taking photos with his camera and got run out of camp in one hell of a hurry. Making good their escape they realised that they could have had their horses stolen, which would have been a major disaster.

In the vicinity of Prince Albert they felled their timber requirements, restricted only by the amount each horse could drag without getting exhausted with a days's travel. The journey back took twice as long, a wide detour being made around the Indian Camp!!

Their next task was to build their sod hut. No planning application was required, no building inspectors to interfere, no rates to pay, all materials readily to hand.

The sods were cut about two feet long, fifteen inches wide and four inches thick. The walls were built like laying bricks with the grass side down. A rough door of split pine logs six feet high and two feet six inches wide was hung from an upright post set in the sod walls. Two glass windows two feet by two feet didn't let in much light but certainly let in the extreme winter frost, despite keeping the stove in all night. In those days dad sported a moustache. On waking some winter mornings, moisture from his breath would freeze his upper lip to the blanket!

Inside the sod hut measured twelve feet wide by twenty-four feet long. Half was curtained off for bedrooms, the remainder used as a kitchen-cum-living room. At eaves level the straight poles, which they had travelled such a vast distance to obtain, were laid from wall to wall. On top was laid tarpaper, then brushwood with a final layer of more cut turf. An iron chimney pot poked through the roof at the far end allowing smoke and fumes to escape from the stove below. Manure from the oxen, mixed with a little water was used to plaster the inside walls. When thoroughly dry from the heat of the stove two coats of lime-wash was applied. In fact, manure from the animals was a valuable commodity. Stacked and dried out during the summer months It was used as winter fuel replacing wood, which was always in short supply.

The house was finished before winter and they moved in, but of course the logs cut that summer were still green and kept shrinking

"The beginning of better times to come"

making many cracks round door and windows that the cold winds crept through. There were times when, outside, the wind roared and howled around the shack, when a blizzard was raging icy flakes of snow drifted in settling on the almost red hot stove only to melt away in seconds. Every morning someone ventured outside for a bucket of snow to melt on the stove for drinking purposes. If one left water in the container overnight, even in the house, it was frozen into a solid lump by day-break.

Winters were long and life monotonous, they played games, and read again and again the few books which they had brought over from England. The women never ventured outside for months on end. This makeshift abode was indeed a poor exchange for my ancestors former grand manor house in Westbrook, Boxford, but my father never complained or voiced any regret at their decision to emigrate.

Dad told the story of one day in February, it was deadly still and calm but towards noon snow began to fall, the wind rose gaining in power and velocity. The blizzard lasted for two days and two nights, great drifts piled against the house and cow barn. Visibility was so bad the buildings couldn't be seen. Yet still the stock had to be fed and watered.

Following a guide rope, dad made for the barn, gave the stock hay with snow to lick because all the water had frozen solid. On the third day the wind dropped, outside the thermometer registered forty five degrees below, the sun shone reflecting the perfect white of the landscape, absolute quiet prevailed, it filled the air, so quiet one could hear the silence.

Somehow man and beast survived that first bitter winter.

The growing season is short - a mere 100 to 105 days. This was virgin ground, land that had never in its history seen a plow or cultivator. Land that had remained untouched since the retreat of the last ice age some twenty thousand years before. The Indian is a hunter, for him there was always food and clothes in plenty from the vast Buffalo herds until those great beasts were decimated almost to extinction by white man's greed. With the arrival of the Chinnock wind spring came with a rush.

Dad's oxen, all responding to a name were broken to pull a wagon, to follow the ups and downs, twists and curves of the trail, not to pull a plow.

"The Virgin Soil"

With a faraway look in his eyes, as though still struggling with his team he'd shake his head, saying, "The capers I had getting those stubborn, cussed animals to pull together, keep in a straight line for half a mile to the end of my section, turn as one and back again all day and every day was just nobody's business". Yet he got a lot of enjoyment watching the moist, dark brown loam soil slide off the mould board and silently roll over upside down.

On a good day he'd walk twelve miles turning over one and a half acres, cutting six inches deep, standing up the furrows almost on end like one did back in Berkshire until a neighbour called one day with sound advice. "You got much to learn young man, you'll grow no wheat in this God damn country if you plows like that, you'll lose all the moisture when the snow melt dries out, you gotta cut that old turf no more than two inches deep, turn the sod over flat, drill your seed next day and keep the roller going."

Every year they broke more prairie until eventually Dad and his brothers' sections were all under cultivation. The land, rich and fertile needed no fertilizer, growing good crops year after year but prices were atrocious and some years they couldn't sell all they produced, being forced to carry stocks over into the next season. They didn't build ricks. The method for harvesting was by stook threshing, hauling the sheaves of corn to the stationary threshing drum. Neighbours lent each other a hand making up a strong gang working from section to section.

Not every harvest was a success, most summers were glorious yet rainfall almost non-existent. After sowing time another hazzard was grasshoppers, it could be a beautiful day, clear and bright, then the sky would darken but no clouds were visible. Soon everything was covered by a green, hopping, wriggling mass. Millions upon millions of insects floating in the air like a cloud, down they would fall and devour every green corn shoot in sight. Then without warning rise on wings to fly to a new field of destruction.

Gophers were another dreadful pest destroying entirely the new crops of grain dad and his brothers had worked so hard to grow. Prairie fires, often caused by electric storms, cyclones and early frosts that freeze the ears of corn, whilst still in the "milk" stage, were just some of the problems those early pioneers had to cope with.

Dad's savings had long been spent, harvest money was a long way off, somehow cash had to be obtained to purchase food and bare essentials. Dad, the only batchelor had no family ties, he rode his horse 150 hard miles to Saskatoon, the nearest large town. Here he shovelled snow off the streets, graded roads and worked as a wiper in the railway station, cleaning and oiling the great locomotives all for a few cents an hour.

Back on the homestead when field work was quiet or non-existent, he told tales of 'whooping it up in town". This was North Battleford, the nearest main settlement, 80 miles away. Three days in the saddle, one day and night in town, then a three-day journey home. Still very much a frontier town, single-storey shops and houses with hitching rails for horses, and unpaved, dusty streets. Homesteaders, tradesmen, travellers and vagabonds crowded the saloons where rye whiskey cost just one dollar a bottle. Cardsharps relieved the unwary of their hard-earned cash and flashy females flaunted their charms.

Drunken brawls were commonplace. The saloon was a focal point in any community, a venue for crooks, loud music and some of the best yarns you'd ever likely to hear.

"Leave your guns at the bar please," said a conspicuous notice over the door as one entered. Another displayed prominently over the bar for all to see never failed to find favour amongst the customers.

A Toast
The Frenchman drinks his native wine.
The German, his lager beer.
The Englishman, his half and half,
Because it gives him cheer.
The Scotsman drinks his whisky neat.
The Irish like it hot.
The Canadian's got no national drink
So he drinks the bloody lot!

In those days my father, in his early thirties, six feet tall, broad shouldered and tough as they come was not a man to be trifled with, although by nature quiet and even tempered.

In one of his infrequent visits to town he bought new clothes including three ties, went to the theatre, luxuriated in a bath, shave and hair cut, smoked cigars which he disliked. In short, he had a wonderful time. Lost the remainder of his money playing fan-tan, roulette, poker and getting involved with a trickster.

I loved to listen to the story of how he finally got the better of this rogue.

In a dark corner of the saloon a crowd surrounded the man as he sat at a low table swiftly manoeuvring three upside-down tin cups.

"Come on stranger" the man calls to my father. "Quickness of the hand deceives the eye. Watch the little pea. Flip, flip, flip, where is she?" "Bet you a level dollar you don't know." My father carefully watched the tins being moved, first one way then the other. "Under that" says dad. "You're quick" said the dealer turning up the cup and showing the pea hidden beneath it. Dad won three times out of the next four throws.

Surely this was easy money as he picked up a dollar each time. With a sly grin the dealer said. "You a gambler, farmer?" "I'll up the stakes - even money, ten dollars each way, I win or you do." It was a foregone conclusion, this time dad lost his money to the amusement of the watching crowd who'd no doubt been caught themselves. Dad rode home determined to get even one day.

A few weeks later, on the last visit to town before spring sowing, he took his brother Doug and a friend. Amongst themselves they had outlined a plan to get the better of the gambler. After a tiring three days in the saddle the three lads made straight for the saloon, tied their mounts loosely to the hitching rail, then casually strode to the bar and ordered drinks.

Sure enough the cheating gambler was still in business, relieving unwary passing strangers of their hard-earned dollars.

"Anyone else wants to win some easy dollars?" "All you gotta do is watch the little pea, come'on lads I'm giving good money away tonight." "Sure, I'll have a go says my father pushing his way through the crowd. The same procedure took place as before. The pea was placed under a tin cup and and all three cups were shuffled around. Dad won three times in a row.

"You're on a winning streak young man, you game to play for a bigger stake?" Bet-ya five to one, ten dollars to my fifty" says the gambler. "Yep, but only if you put your money on the table," dad replied. Dad's two accomplices had quietly moved into position, one on either side of the gambler's table on which sixty dollars had been placed. There was tension in the small crowd of onlookers who knew that my father was on a loser. The dealer swiftly spread out the tins again and said viciously. "Now then farmer where is she?" "Under this one says dad." Picking up the middle cup. At the same instance down came a big hand from either side onto the other two cups, all three were lifted together. There was no pea under either, no way could my father have won. What happened next took place in seconds.

"Reckon you owe me this," says my father grabbing the pile of dollar bills, in the same movement he lifted the table pushing the gambler over in a medley of arms, legs, tin cups and the little pea which had been held between the gambler's right thumb and forefinger. The three made a dive for the swing doors before two tough bouncers could bar their way. In a single stride they cleared the sidewalk, in another bound they were in the saddle and away at full gallop down the dark, deserted street to disappear in the limitless prairie,

Just before the First World War my father made the decision that was to change the history of our branch of the family. He'd return to England and if possible set up farming in the land of his birth, where the climate was kinder and one's neighbours lived just around the corner. He worked his return passage on a tramp ship, he had no money and only the clothes he stood up in. What he did have was a wealth of experience and a tiny block of land in the centre of Canada.

My late Uncles were to farm this land for the next ten or twelve years until my father finally sold out. A legal document was drawn up between the purchasers, two brothers named Sitz and my father, the details of which make interesting reading and I am proud to have it in my possession.

My father honestly thought he was on to a good thing, by now firmly established and farming back in England, he could sit back in the certain belief that the proceeds from his Canadian holding would arrive in his bank account on the appointed day each year through the agreed half-crop payment.

Carefully reading the agreement through one would think that every possible clause had been covered, nothing could possibly go wrong.

In fact it didn't work out like that. Most years the crops failed for one reason or another - or so the Sitz brothers implied. Then the bottom dropped out of everything in the 1929 slump. My father never received a single payment for the homestead he had sweated and slaved to create from bare, virgin, wind-swept prairie.

Totally disillusioned with the whole affair, in 1936 he did a deal with his brother Douglas, swapping the worthless paper agreement for a single building plot on the Bath Road between Newbury and Thatcham, which he later sold for sixty pounds to a developer.

Three years later with the outbreak of the Second World War, grain prices started moving on an upward spiral. Payments for the land started to come through and within four years Uncle Doug received all the monies due, including interest dating back to 1925!

There was no point in father complaining. A deal is a deal as they say.

In 1985 on my fourth visit to Canada I made the pilgrimage to Dad's former homestead retracing his trek west across that vast land, but I travelled in luxury on the Trans-Canadian National Railway. Getting off the train at Unity, a tiny village community in the middle of nowhere, with unpaved, dusty roads, a small cluster of wooden houses and the inevitable grain elevators that stand alongside all prairie rail stations.

I hitched a lift to the homestead, twelve and a half miles west of Unity and twelve miles south. Dad's quarter section is now part of a larger holding farmed by Mr Gerald Deck, his wife and six children. They made me very welcome and I stayed with them for some six

"The Homestead today in Winter"

days enjoying their kind hospitality,

Driving an ancient station wagon Gerald drove me along a dusty track, flanked on either side by ripening crops of wheat that wouldn't be sneered at back in England. In one corner of the huge field a small patch of rough uncultivated ground marks the site of the old homestead, with the sod house and barns now long gone all that remains are a few trees planted by my father to gain some slight shelter from the relentless wind.

I stood transfixed in silence trying to comprehend those days of long ago, when my father first arrived in this spot and how he had broken this land for the first time in history, taming this small hunk of the earth's surface.

I asked myself, "What was the driving force that had prompted my ancestors to leave the beautiful Lambourn Valley, so peaceful and tranquil to eke out a living in this far distant land?"

To my Father and Grandparents - with great love - without whose courage to emigrate I might never have seen this great land.

Westbrook old manor The home they left behind

Broad Acres

Across the valley from Mousefield Farm (my home for many years) is another farm called Red Farm which came on the market in 1957. After much thought and prolonged negotiations with the owner I purchased this 107 acre block of fertile land with its picturesque range of brick and tile buildings. I planned to use most of this extra land for grain production. Thirty acres of winter wheat, forty-eight acres of spring barley, just two fields! Never before had I grown grain on such a scale. No comparison of course with the barley barons of the Lambourn Valley or the Berkshire Downs, nevertheless to myself, if not my father, it was a huge acreage especially when it came to ploughing a forty-eight acre block with a Fordson tractor and two-furrow trailer plough!

Drilled mid-October, come Christmas the wheat looked promising, if anything a bit 'winter-proud' caused by the mild weather we had enjoyed to date, but sharp late frosts and a biting east wind the following March quickly set the crop back a peg,

I dilly-dallied over the question to top dress, perhaps a hundredweight of nitrogen to the acre, but decided that I couldn't afford the extra cost, short-sighted policy I know, but I was already in serious debt to the bank for the purchase of the farm. The barley went in well that first spring, but the second-hand 13 Coulter corn drill, which I had purchased from a dispersal sale for £50 was almost too much for Teddie, my ageing Standard Fordson to pull.

'Redlands' was the name we had given to our largest field. A particular feature is two sand-capped hills both with sharp inclines, only by drilling anti-clockwise, so as to approach by the lesser slope could the tractor pull the laden corn drill to the summit, even then the operator riding the drill had to jump off the footplate and push. It is surprising how 150 lbs less weight and one man-power at the rear made all the difference between success or failure in riding the crest.

Teddie belched black, sooty smoke into the cloudless blue sky as he staggered over the top, quickly gaining speed on the down-hill stretch leaving the drill-man to race after and jump on the swaying, bouncing footboard. Once we levelled out, a quick check on seed and fertiliser raised doubts whether we would make it round the large headland to our refill point on the far side, where fresh supplies awaited us on an old fourwheeled trailer, which I had constructed by stripping the bodywork and engine from a pre First World War Sunbeam motor car, then building a flatbed onto the strongly made chassis. With its red painted, wooden spoked wheels this fine piece of antiquity still gives useful service in 1988.

That spring nature smiled graciously upon our newly acquired acres, within ten days of sowing long, straight lines of bright green barley shoots pointed skywards. Pee-wits ran quietly between the rows leading the intruder away from the four pear-shaped, stone-coloured eggs before taking flight, their wings making a noise like a fan as they beat the air, calling their loud pee-wit, pee-wit as they circled round and feigned attack leaving one in no doubt that the farmer is only sharing this small piece of England with other occupiers.

My eldest son Michael, although not destined for an agricultural career was a useful tractor driver even at the tender age of ten years. After a day at school he volunteered to drive the tractor pulling a light-weight triple-gang Cambridge Roller. On our sandy loam it was essential to consolidate it if one wished to conserve moisture.

Now that I considered myself a grain farmer I obtained every pamphlet pertaining information on chemical weed killers that I could lay my hands on.

M.C.P.A. killed most annual weeds. I decided it was prudent to spend a bit of money if it meant weeds would be kept under control, unfortunately this particular chemical had no effect on couch grass. The long creeping rhizomes had long enjoyed freedom in the light soils of Red Farm. If the growing season turned out to be a wet one, our crop of volunteer couch was often as tall as the procter barley, making for difficult harvest conditions. Dora the dairymaid stoutly maintained that our barley straw was far superior to any purchased from neighbours due to the fact that there was plenty of "rubbish" in the bales, often with the smell of first class hay!! The battle against couch was finally won when my sons took over in 1976. Sprayed the crops with 'Round-up' and grew maize for fodder feeding.

With expanding acres, so the number of commercial travellers seemed to multiply selling everything from stockholm tar, for the treatment of lame cows, to some new patent drench that smelt strongly of whisky and was guaranteed to cure every bovine ailment. On a crisp, bright morning in early April a dapper little man puffed his way up the rutted farm track on a bicycle. Cycle clips held his trousers tight above the ankles, loud check sports jacket and a soft peaked cap completed his attire. His saddle-bag stuffed full of leaflets and what looked like an ample supply of refreshments.

With the gift of a born salesman, he claimed to be selling a brand new crop sprayer for the ridiculous price of £45. With a 50 gallon capacity, a 30 foot folding boom, two sets of nozzles for both high and low volume spraying and a pump to create enough pressure to give complete crop cover from the spray cones. The catch was one had to agree to use their chemicals for a minimum of five years!

Listening intently to his prattle I'm sure he was convinced he'd made a sale until I tactfully pointed out to him that my pre-war tractor didn't have the necessary hydraulic lift and three point linkage for attachment of a sprayer. No problem, no problem at all, he would hire me a Fergie tractor for a few days, he explained that he had an arrangement with Martin & Chillingsworth in London Road, Newbury. I took up the offer, sprayed all my grain crop in two days with great success and in due course got another fifteen years use out of that special offer purchased from a salesman on a bicycle!!

Blessed with an optimistic nature I share the countryman's inherent belief in a Higher Power, without this certain faith, no matter how good the soil or how fine the man made equipment that after the seed is sown, the plant will germinate and grow to maturity no man should plant one seed.

The summer passed without any great weather disasters, we missed the heavy thunderstorms that often twists and flattens a promising crop.

Our first big harvest would soon be ripe. Ears hung heavy with grain, gentle summer breezes sent wave like ripples across the golden

The passing of an era. Our last rick

acres. A huge flock of noisy sparrows swooped down from the hedgerow every day to feast. Rooks and pigeons had battered down another section half the size of a football pitch. Rabbits, despite constant persecution from shotguns, wires and gin traps had managed to dine handsomely off something like four acres, however enough was left for me to worry how we were going to harvest the remainder. Our small acreage on the home farm had, until a few years previous, still been harvested with our No 5 Albion Binder, a horse drawn model converted to go behind the tractor. Having decided that whilst picturesque, corn ricks were a thing of the past, my father and I went 'shopping', purchasing a six foot cut Massey trailer combine. Equipped with a six cylinder TVO engine this only drove the cutter bar and threshing mechanism, even so it was all 'Teddie' could do to pull this great red monster round the field especially in a wet summer, when wheels sunk six inches or more in the soft soil.

It was of course a 'bagger' combine harvester. Roy Adnams our farm lad at the time drove the tractor. I was on 'sacks', perched on a tiny platform six foot by three high above the cut stubble. A safety bar prevented the operator from stepping into space. Except for the fact that one was on the move, albeit rather slowly, one's task on the platform was exactly the same as on the old stationary threshers. It was hard, continuous work, the golden grain poured out of little trap doors into hessian sacks. Two 'shoots' for best grain, one for 'seconds' and a fourth for weed seeds. With the mouth of a sack clamped at each outlet, the operator pulled a piece of binder twine cut to the correct length, from a conveniently placed bundle, unclamped the full sack, shook the sack with hands and bent knees to settle the grain, folded the top of the sack with three inch overlaps, tied it twice round tightly with string, lifted the full sack of grain (now weighing some two hundred-weight - 224 lbs) to a sloping ramp at the rear where the sack slid to the ground and hopefully didn't burst open on impact. No time to lose, no chance to admire the country scene or our beautiful valley. Quickly place another empty sack from the rack into position before the next one is full and the whole mad process repeated. With grain 'running' well it was a race against time. Often I prayed for a blockage so that I could catch up and perhaps get a gulp of lemonade from a grubbie bottle to wash the choking dust down!

My father liked to keep a close watch on our progress, he'd stroll across the cut stubble to meet us as we turned the corner of uncut corn. His well-worn trilby hat pushed back on his forehead. I was never too busy that I didn't stop for a few minutes chat. Weather wise, his forecast of weather to come was often more accurate than the professionals. Scooping a handful of grain from a nearby sack he'd examine the sample minutely in the palm of his hand, then put a few grains in his mouth biting them in half, testing for hardness and grain quality. Like a connoisseur sampling fine wine before giving his opinion on our years work. "I reckon you got a malting sample here me boy. Pay to get a quote from Doltons and sell, money in the bank, would stop that bank manager breathing down your neck.

You could buy some feed barley through the winter in dribs and drabs as and when you want it."

On a good day we harvested five acres by the time rising dew stopped play. However work for the day was far from over. I was not into corn growing in a big enough way to warrant the expense of a grain dryer. I found that providing one harvested whilst the sun shone and moisture content did not exceed 18%, grain stored in sacks kept quite well for up to three months.

A yield of two tons to the acre meant that one hundred full sacks of grain scattered around on the stubble had to be man-handled on to the tractor trailer and transported to the big barn, where we had laid timbers on the concrete floor to protect the filled sacks of corn from rising damp.

Although this humping of sacks, after a long day on the combine harvester was exhausting, nevertheless it was still a family affair. Returning to the barn with a full load, workers and children sat atop the bags of grain, still warm from the heat of the day, singing their hearts out, as the blood-red sun sank behind Brickiln Wood. No electric light in the barn. In fact power didn't arrive until as late as 1989. Lanterns hung from the rafters casting a faint glow on ruddy sweat covered features of both young and not so young!

Never once did we fail to clear the day's yield working far into the night, often by the reflected sunlight of the harvest moon. Returning for the last load it was not unusual to give a rude awakening to our partridge stock which had settled down for the night in some slight hollow.

Partridge invariably roost, or more correctly 'jig' in a small covey out in the open, well away from hedge or cover and lie close together in a loose circle, heads turned outwards. If disturbed they scatter in all directions, fooling the intruder, as well as avoiding collision amongst themselves.

"Our first self-propelled combine harvester"

With the day's harvest safely in the dry we made our weary way home, often in the small hours. I always made a point of removing my boots before getting into bed, hardly worth removing much clothing, soon be six am, milking time once more.

The trailer combine harvester gave several years of faithful service, but now I was growing over one hundred acres of cereals each season, the situation desperately needed a more modern machine. I purchased from South Berks Agricultural Company, at Hermitage, a Massey self-propelled 8 foot cut bagger for the sum of £625. An outrageous outlay of capital. Previously it had completed six seasons on Woodrows Farm, Aldworth. Possessing no hydraulic lifts, all adjustments to table, sails etc were hand operated. The engine started on petrol before switching over to TVO, when warm.

With all going well there was great satisfaction listening to the pleasant snip, snip, snip of the knife cutting a great swathe through swaying waves of ripe golden grain. The steady, reassuring hum of the drum as it separated corn from straw. Occasionally there would be a loud whrum'm'm from deep within the machine as a wad of barley and damp couch grass hit the digestive system. Terrified rabbits made a bolt for cover, a hen pheasant, reluctant to fly ran in front of the knife her brood of half-grown chicks struggled to hold the pace. Way up ahead a big dog fox made for the safety of the boundary hedge, annoyed by this mean disturbance of his world.

One sat on a comfortable armchair-like seat high above the roaring engine, surrounded by an array of hand levers, foot pedals, and switches. Thick, throat clogging dust rose upwards from the cutting knife. On hot, sunny days a large proportion of this dust and chaff settled on the red hot manifold below and on many occasions I had to make a smart exit to avoid scorched pants when the engine burst into flames! Finally, some years later the whole blooming outfit went up in an inferno of flames and black smoke, from burning rubber tyres, taking with it the last two acres of uncut grain!

It is not much use lamenting progress. Today's farmer, with his moisture-meter, his pocket calculator, his CB radio and his computer, is a far cry from his ancestors. Gone are the binders, the stooks, the ricks, the threshing days. When all the boys in the village enjoyed ratting. The finished ricks stood proud to the evening sky, now its straw filled plastic bags which shine black to the setting sun.

Harvest time is not the fun it was.

Bale Cart

'If hay is fit to bale its fit to stack' - so the saying goes. However, our hay, carted from the field by tractor and trailer was stacked in the great old barn at Mousefield. This ancient traditional timber and tiled roofed building was originally built to store sheaves of corn to be threshed out in winter by hand flail. Each summer, if we had had a good hay harvest, the bales would be stacked to the very top of the barn. Way up amongst the massive oak beams, spiders and our resident bats.

To get the last bales right to the apex, we swung them up by ropes on block and tackle. What a laborious task that was, one bale at a time, and golly, didn't we sweat on hot summer days, there was just no air up there, under the roof tiles.

We dare not fill the barn too quickly, just put a load or two in each day. Giving each layer of hay time to sweat out a little. Fire from internal combustion was always a danger. To allow air to circulate freely between the stacked bales we left some narrow tunnels, this was a great help to dry the sap from new made hay. Unfortunately, it gave lovely nesting places for our free range hens. We found a large proportion of these eggs whilst still fresh, but many remained hidden until finally discovered in spring as our store of hay finally vanished down hungry cows' stomachs. The farmyard boasted two or three fine mature roosters, who always did their stuff, and there are few more satisfactory sights than a proud mother hen appearing one spring morning with her brood of multi-coloured chicks.

Ten, maybe fifteen years ago, say in the early 1970's, I would have said that hay baling and the transport of the bales couldn't progress any further. How wrong I was!

Today in the 1990s bales, and big round ones at that, are moved from meadow to livestock use untouched by hand! We had an intermediate stage using a conventional baler and a Macconnel bale packer, one of the few ever used in this area. An unwieldy piece of machinery costing us some £5,000. Nevertheless, tagging along behind the baler it gobbled up hay or straw bales by the thousand, and in a mystic arrangement of levers, springs, wheels and heavy duty baler twine usually, but not always, managed to tie a pack of twenty bales. The whole ponderous outfit moving slowly round the field, occasionally parturition occurred rather like an elephant giving birth!

These days we don't make hay, my sons can't cope with the fickleness of the English climate. We baled and wrapped silage for the first time in 1986. Excellent job. Round straw bales are stacked outside pyramid fashion. The round bales shed rain like feathers on a duck's back, we get little wastage and these are moved two at a time on steel spikes as and when required.

The Albourne Moonrakers

By the mid 1930's many of the Berkshire dairy farmers were changing over to the black and white friesians. Big framed cows which gave a lot of milk, but of rather poor quality. With only two or two and a half percent butterfat. If you were putting this milk on the train to some London dairy, it didn't matter, we were not paid on butterfat content. But the farmers wives would complain it took too much milk to make a few lbs. of butter, and they had to add some artificial colouring to make it look respectable. They would say to their husbands: "If you want your family to have some decent cream and butter, you'd better get on to Frank Houghton, get him to "find us a Guernsey house-cow."

So dad would get a post card. "Can you find me a genuine fresh calver for the house." Our main source of supply was Charlie Hale of Albourne, one of the straightest and most honest farmers I was privileged to know. A real old fashioned Wiltshire countryman. Although Albourne is only just over the Berkshire border, the accent of the country folk is completely different from ours.

A letter would be sent off to Charlie stating our requirements. Almost by return post the answer was: "I can fix you up Frank, I've a couple of cows just calved in. We've got some heifers due shortly so I can spare the cows, and we have plenty of milk for the round at present. I remember my first journey down to Albourne with dad. Even our old Ford van enjoyed that trip, for one thing it is flat all the way. Out of Newbury on the old Bath Road, we were soon at Hungerford, leaving the A4 one soon crosses the River Kennet, then through the picturesque village of Chilton Foliat, it didn't take us long to reach Albourne. Entering this small country town, we pass on our right a stone and brick built barn with the figure of a man leaning on his spade. He seems to have just stepped out of his conical shelter, and at the same time indicates the wind direction; a very unusual weathervane. On earlier visits to Albourne with my grandfather, he had told me fascinating stories about this gardener's powers to predict the weather.

Charlie's Farm, almost in the centre of the village was always kept immaculate and he thought the world of his Guernsey Cows. On our journey down, dad had said, "Charlie, as got two cows to sell. We've only an order for one, if we buy both we keep tuther'un ourselves, push our milk up a bit, put a dash of colour in it too!" Charlie seemed pleased to see us. Always a friendly man, shaking dad's hand, he did the same for me. "Breaking your son in early then Frank, I see. Like a good hoss, it pays to start them young." He leads the way to a loose box. Inside standing side by side, tethered with a chain around their necks, are two smart, well-groomed Channel Island milch cows, both freshly calved. As we enter, the nearest cow turns to gaze with large brown docile eyes. I couldn't help but notice her immensely long eyelashes, well over an inch in length, but these wouldn't be adding anything to their value, it would be their milking potential that would set the price.

Moving up to the first cow and giving her a gentle tap, Charlie says: "Come'on then gel, show yer'self." Bending down he reaches for two of the cows teats, standing stiffly out from her extended udder. Expertly, he pulls a continuous stream of rich creamy milk which runs down the concrete floor in a frothy cascade to the drain. "This one's got a nice heifer calf, Frank, I shan't want to part wean, but tuther'un's got a bull calf." "I'll be chucking him in the deal to help pay transport."

My father casts an expert eye over both cows. Inspects their eyes to see if they are bright and alert, the nose which should be damp and dewy, a sign of good health. A nice straight back ending in a slim tail correctly set in place. In turn dad runs his hand along each cow's back, then grasps a solid handful of the cows hide just behind the shoulder. This should be soft, pliable and silky to the touch, and lift easily from the flesh beneath. Next inspecting the udder, which should come well up behind under her tail, also well forward with nicely shaped teats placed squarely on each corner.

Drawing each quarter to test how easy she drew milk, the last thing we required was a hard milker, especially as it may well be a farmer's wife who would be milking a house-cow. Dad now squirts a sample of milk into the palm of his weather beaten hand. He does each teat in turn, looking for any sign of mastitus, at the same time he feels with thumb and fore-finger, for any sign of a "pea". This is a warty growth in the teat channel that can seriously interrupt the flow of milk.

At the time I didn't fully appreciate the accumulation of knowledge I was building up from working closely with my father.

"How many calves they had then Charlie?" Pointing to the big, wellgrown cow which was busily licking her calf tied up short by her head, Charlie replies: "She's a third calver, Frank, her'll give 'e five gallons a day, and keep it up too. Fact oh matter is, us had a job to dry her off last back end. T'other un's only a second calver and she calved young first time." Dad steps up between the two cows, grasps the horn of the younger cow, pulling her head round and up. Thumb and finger of his free hand is inserted in her nostrils. Leaving go of the horn, he now pulls back the cows lower lip and inspects her teeth. "You're right, Charlie, she's only got six teeth up, and the two calf teeth are still there." Charlie continues to extol the merits of his stock. "That cow's got all her life in front on 'er, her's a good'un snoo Frank."

"Well, you two have had a good look at 'em, 'ow much you going to give I for 'em, chuck the bull calf in mind?." "You haven't had a wasted journey, I never shows you a bad 'un." Dad paused in thought, the next move was up to him. "Yes, they're two grand cows, Charlie. I'm going to offer you fifty-six pounds for the two, that's twenty-eight pounds apiece. Couldn't give such a good price if we hadn't got a customer lined up for one of them." "We'll milk the other ourselves. Make the journey more worthwhile if we take the two." Charlie seems pleased with the offer, but like all farmers he is out to strike the best deal he can get. "You always bin fair with I, Frank, but you'll have to spring a mite more yet."

Dad replies, "Or right Charlie, give us a pound back for luck and I'll give you sixty quid the pair." Once more the familiar smack of hands and the deal is sealed. "Look after 'em till day after tomorrow, Charlie, I"ll get Bob Evans to collect them in his truck. Make sure they're loaded quiet, won't you? Ole Bob is a bit of a tare ass if he's got a lot of work on." "Sure, I'll look after 'em same as if they were still me own." Dad takes out his cheque book. If he made a deal he always paid before leaving, a fact greatly appreciated by the farming fraternity.

Driving home again we discuss our purchase. Dad seems well

pleased. "Fred Kimber of Cold Ash Farm, our customer for a house cow, should be well pleased with the older cow, we will get Bob Evans to drop the cow with the bull calf off at our place before going on to Fred's farm" says dad. "Best if he doesn't know we bought two, or he'll only think we kept the best cow for ourselves. Reckon we cah charge him thirtyeight pound for her delivered. Bob will want a couple of pounds to bring 'em back from Aldbourne. I'm sure Fred will be more than pleased with her, she draws well and looks like giving a lot of milk. He takes a bit of satisfying though, he's a fussy ole devil."

I did note that on more than one occasion, dad and I would praise our new purchase up to such an extent that the price we intended to charge would rise several pounds on the journey!

The young cow joined our herd, her milk was rich, creamy and a nice deep colour. My mother would separate the cream with our Lister Separator. At the end of the week she would make some lovely farmhouse butter in the end-over-end butter churn.

The bull-calf stayed on its mother drinking all the milk it wanted. By the time it was eight weeks old, it was a real 'vealer'. Good enough for dad to sell to Liddiard's, the butcher on the bridge in Northbrook Street. He got ten pounds for it.

The story Charlie liked to tell us on our visits:-

On certain clear nights of the full moon, after turn out time from the pub, a group of the locals would gather round the village pond, armed with hayracks, their bellies full of beer, they would see who could be the first to rake the moon out of the water! From what I can gather it usually resulted in a ducking for some and on a frosty night a quick way to sober up!! 'The moonrakers of Aldbourne'

The Family Car

Childhood memories are always the best of course, and those take me back to the horse and cart days, but the motor car has been part of our farm scene, since I was knee-high to a grasshopper, as the saying goes.

I guess that I was about ten years old when my father - a person who liked to move with the times - purchased a Model T Ford. My mother was furious at the time and threatened never to ride in such a contraption. She did of course capitulate and sat in front, bolt upright, next to father when he drove into town on market day. She always maintained that she never felt safe in the noisy thing and on descending any steep hill she would always get out and walk, in case the brakes failed and the vehicle ran away. Another fear was that the whole lot would erupt in flames. "You sure you haven't got the brake on Frank, I can smell rubber?" she often asked anxiously.

The Ford was not the first mechanised vehicle my father owned. In his bachelor days he drove a motor bike and sidecar but this was short-lived. He told the story that one day, rounding a sharp, blind bend he was suddenly confronted by a ten ton steam roller. Instead of applying the brake he accidently pushed the throttle lever, with the result that his precious bike was totally wrecked in the collision and dad shot over the handlebar to land in a water-filled ditch. This was a lucky escape from certain death because the roller passed over the bike reducing dad's prized possession to a flattened mass of twisted metal!

My father drove around the local countryside for many years in the Model T, although my mother much preferred to travel by horse and trap. I cannot remember what happened to this vehicle in the end. It would be a nice surprise if one day it reappeared, hidden away in the back of one of our old barns or discovered overgrown with brambles and nettles amongst our collection of discarded farm machinery, but I fear there will be no such luck! The next family car was a Clyno. It was simply just a square box with a wheel at each corner. Under the bonnet a tiny four cylinder petrol engine capable of transporting four adults at thirty-five miles per hour on level ground, but uphill one felt that all the passengers should get out and push. I don't think many of these cars were made because I cannot recall ever seeing another model on the road or in any car museum.

Misfortune struck one Sunday morning on a day out to visit my aunt and uncle who live at Wingfield in Somerset. This was a major excursion in those days, a return journey of over one hundred miles. My father drove, mother sat in the passenger seat nursing my baby sister. Squeezed into the tiny back seat, like sardines in a tin sat my maternal grandparents and myself. Almost at journey's end whilst negotiating a sharp bend in the town of Trowbridge, dad lost control, crossed the white line and crashed head-on into another car travelling in the opposite direction. Luckily cars didn't speed quite so much in those early days of motoring.

Both cars were written off, but fortunately the only human casualty was grandfather Perris who ruined his trilby hat and cut his head rather badly on the interior roof light! Whatever he was doing wearing headgear in such cramped conditions I cannot imagine. I can recall the men standing in the centre of the street locked in argument over who was in the wrong. My mother and grandmother sobbing on the pavement and worrying over Aunt Dorie's hot lunch being overcooked. A telegram broke the sad news to our intended hosts of the mishap. Eventually we caught a train back to Newbury. The wrecked car was towed away by the local scrap dealer.

Next came an Austin Seven, not much larger than a pram, nevertheless a four seater! My father stood over six feet tall. How he ever succeeded in squeezing his large frame into such a small space, I never knew.

On a hot, thundery day in late summer he had driven to a farm beyond the village of Yattendon to purchase cattle. By seven o'clock in the evening he had failed to return home. "Wherever can your father be at this time of the night?" asked my mother anxiously. It was almost dark when he was spotted walking up the garden path carrying a bag of tools. It transpired that was all that was left intact of his car. Now, I look back with pride. What a courageous man my father was. Unruffled, calm as ever he explained the situation and the sad demise of yet another car.

Rounding a bend in the road at the foot of Everington Hill, dad spotted a heavily laden lorry as it crested the top. The road in those days was single track, instead of slowing down as expected the lorry gathered speed, the driver leaning out of the cab window frantically waving his arm in a signal for my father to reverse, but there was not time, with the result that he sat in the driving seat awaiting the inevitable crash. When it came the car was pushed backwards some fifty yards ending up in a thick, thorny roadside hedge with the lorry on the bonnet. From the wreck my father stepped out unhurt, but very annoyed with the lorry driver, a cockney market trader on his way back to London with a load of potatoes.

"Sorry mate, I missed me gears and I got no brakes worth anything." Later enquiries were to prove this unscrupulous character had no fixed address and no money. His vehicle was on hire purchase and uninsured and you can't get blood from a stone.

Subsequently the Austin Seven was sold for thirty shillings!

There is an old saying "What you never have you never miss". But this proverb works the other way too. Once one becomes motorised it is difficult to manage without a car. My father was like a cowboy without a horse, so it was not long before he was on the lookout for another vehicle.

A well known local farmer, who shall remain nameless, had gone bankrupt. The cause had been the usual combination of high living, fast women and slow race horses. The bank foreclosed with the result that the farmer's live and dead stock came under the hammer. My father seldom missed a farm sale always optimistic that there would be bargains.

At this particular sale he purchased the unfortunate gentleman's Rover car for seven pounds ten shillings. When new it was an expensive and luxurious vehicle. Roomy, it sat five adults in comfort, with comfortable seats in real leather and a highly polished mahogany dashboard decorated with rows of dials and switches. Huge brass headlamps lit the road at night for a hundred yards and more and if any cyclist or pedestrian strayed into its path the hoot from a massive horn protruding through the windscreen soon cleared the path, quite a contrast to the little Austin Seven. High above the road my parents sat up front, my sister and I in the rear. Dad was sure proud of his 'new' car, and as he said, "From up here I can keep an eye on my neighbour's stock and crops as I drive around the countryside." This robust 16 HP forerunner of the Range Rover would probably never have passed an MOT but when dad drove it, it passed everything else on the King's Highway except petrol stations!! But father kept this fact quiet when in the company of friends.

We had this car for many years and it was the one I learnt to drive on, long before my 17th birthday. It finished its days on the land, very degrading for a car of such standing. We fitted an attachment onto the front bumper to which was fastened a wide wooden hay sweep. What fun that was, to race out to the far corner of the meadow with the tines of the huge sweep bouncing over the green turf, then swing around to collect the sweet smelling hay from the windrows before roaring back to the rickyard with a full load, where a poor labourer sweated his guts out forking the tangled mess onto the petrol driven elevator. This piece of machinery quickly lifted the hay to the rick top where my father and another hired man built the stack which was winter rations for the dairy herd.

When the faithful Rover returned to plain field work, I took every opportunity to practise my driving skills, under the disguise of doing useful farm jobs, one of which was tearing around the meadows dragging a set of chain harrows. This necessitated the purchase of a replacement family car.

On August 20th, 1953 my father purchased from Martin & Chillingworth's showroom in London Road, an Austin A70 for the sum of £679. He hitched a lift into town on market day with one of his cronies, after the business of the day was completed, stock bought and sold, and no doubt well fortified with food and drink, he drove himself home in the first new vehicle he had ever bought. We all had to march out to the front gate to admire this latest automobile, gleaming black it looked very smart. "There will be room to stretch our legs in this car mother", said dad proudly, patting the bonnet and wiping away an imaginary speck of dust with his handkerchief. It was not until he drove it into the garage that he realised he had a problem. Although the front bumper was up against the wall the back of the car protruded some three feet into the drive! There was just no way he could close the garage door! "What are you going to do about that?" asked my mother sarcastically. "The last time you left the garage doors open the wind blew the roof off, if you remember!" Dad solved this problem by knocking a large hole in the brickwork to allow the bonnet of his brand new car to protrude outside, into the forthcoming winter snow and ice!

Unfortunately, this car was to be my father's last, he drove it thousands and thousands of miles up until his sudden death on July 23rd, 1963. He died in harness so to speak. Now he has gone, leaving a gap which it seemed can never be filled.

In 1931 when motor cars were thin on the road, my mother had learnt to drive, but she didn't take kindly to mechanical transport and never really enjoyed motoring. It was a blessing that she kept up her driving licence over the years because she would never have passed any driving test.

Bravely, after my father died she sold the Austin A70 for £100 and purchased an Austin 1100 taking to the road once more after over 30 years. She continued to drive herself into town and on country jaunts with her friends well after her eightieth birthday. I have no doubt that she would have continued driving up to her death in her 90th year if it hadn't been for an unfortunate accident in which she was the innocent party. Whilst driving round the notorious Robin Hood roundabout, accompanied by her lady companion Miss Woods, the car was suddenly and unkindly pushed from behind by the local fire engine, blue lights flashing, siren blaring as it sped on its way to a fire.

The first I knew of this calamity was when I received a telephone call from the Police. "Two elderly ladies were stranded on the grass centre of the Robin Hood roundabout, one of which they understood was my mother. They were very shocked and distraught but otherwise unhurt, the car was a write off but it could be towed away, could I deal with the situation?"

Looking back, perhaps this accident was a blessing in disguise. My mother never drove again, she may have carried on driving too long with more serious results for all concerned,

The first car I owned was a Vauxhall. It is so long ago I cannot remember the model number. Having decided that as I was shortly to be married, some independent means of transport would be needed to take my young bride on honeymoon. The only details I can really recall about that car was that it had big headlights, lots of polished chrome and although it had previously only had one owner it was quite old and the speedo was on the second time round. However, after our wedding and the reception, which was held for a small number of friends and relatives at the Gatehouse Hotel, Reading, on September 28th 1946, my new wife and I set off for Paignton in sunny Devon. Relieved at having made a reasonably unscathed exit from over-enthusiastic wedding guests, we were speeding merrily through the undulating spaces of Salisbury Plain on the A303 when for no apparent reason the car's engine misfired a time or two before packing up completely. "Blast the car, to break down out here in the middle of nowhere, was a fine kettle of fish," I thought to myself. I wasn't courting now so there was no need to fain a breakdown on a lonely road! I got out of the car and lifted the bonnet. "Is it serious dear?" enquired my new spouse leaning out of the side window from the passenger seat. "I dun'no really, there is no smoke, the engine's not overheating and we've still got fuel and water."

I'm not mechanically minded, I had few tools with me and a wedding suit is not the most practical attire for work on a broken down motor vehicle. However, after removing and cleaning the plugs, checking the points and tinkering about with the carburettor, I wiped my hands on a clean handkerchief before returning to the driving seat. To my surprise when I turned the ignition the engine fired and started. On the move once more but with many miles to travel I had doubts about reaching the coast that evening, so a few more miles down the road we turned left for the little Wiltshire town of Mere.

Our wedding night was spent at the Ship Hotel. Next day even though it was on Sunday, I managed to persuade a friendly garage mechanic to check the engine. Twenty-four hours later than planned we made our destination!

Cars don't last for ever, certainly not farmers cars which are subjected to daily travel over rutted gravel tracks. Rainwater, mud and cow manure have disasterous effects on bodywork and I'm afraid in my case lack of general maintenance did little to prolong my cars working lives. I knew that petrol, oil and water were essential ingredients for mobility but after that livestock care came first, I'm afraid.

The Vauxhall and I parted company. No tears were shed. Next came a Morris of which I remember very little except that it didn't cost me much money at the time. I was at a farm sale and although the auctioneer tried all his powers of persuasion he failed to get a bid from the surrounding crowd, On the spur of the moment I said, "£50 sir". No-one else spoke a word. Down came the hammer, I had bought a car and didn't even know if it would start! As things turned out it was not a bad buy and gave good service for a couple of years until I sold it for £132.10.0d in part exchange for a Morris Oxford Saloon. The only new car I have ever purchased in my life.

HJB 896 was the registration number. The price £510.0.0d plus purchase tax £284.16.8d. Delivery charge and petrol £5.8.8d. Total £800.5.4d. The agents, Stradlings Ltd, Northbrook Street, Newbury. It lasted me thirteen long years, I wish now that I had kept it, it was a peach of a car and had a personality all of its own.

The main reason for the disposal of the Morris Oxford was that it was just not large enough to accommodate our growing family on the annual holiday, everything except the kitchen sink was transported either in the car or on the roof!

A friend of mine jokingly suggested nothing short of a bus would be the answer. This was certainly something I hadn't thought of, but came out against the idea when I realised fuel consumption would be excessive and city parking a problem.

In the end I settled for a shooting brake resplendent with wood panelling and ample seating room. On my weekend off duty from the milking chore I often took the whole family on some jaunt. Mystery tours to secluded parts of the Downs, Windsor Great Park or the grassy banks of the River Thames. Sometimes further afield to Exmoor or Dartmoor where the children could really 'let off steam'.

I love to recall one laughable incident that happened just as we were all about to leave the farmhouse on such an expedition. The shooting brake, parked at the front door and loaded with goodies was ready to roll. At this critical moment a car came up the farm drive, stopped and out jumped a rep - all smiles and obviously eager to make a sale. Of all things, he was selling Ceylon tea, superior to any tea one could buy in the shops. It came in bulk, packed and sealed in what he called proper tea boxes. He placed great emphasis on the savings that could be made by purchasing tea in bulk. He suggested I may even be able to pass some on to my farming friends at a profit! At that moment out of the house came five of my children, laughing and squealing in delight at the prospect of going on a picnic. The rep was taken aback for a moment, then he said. "Goodness me Mr Houghton, these aren't all your children are they?" "Oh no," says I "there are two more somewhere!!"

I bought a crate of tea, just to get rid of him, and I admit it was a good buy after all, the only snag was we drank tea for breakfast, lunch, dinner and many many occasions in between.

In an effort not to bore my readers suffice to say that my next vehicle, an Austin Maxi, was purchased as an ex-demonstration model. In fact over a six-year period I had three of these cars, changing the old one every two years. The only criticism I had with them was that the gear selection was not their best feature but they were quite economical to run and had enough power under the bonnet to tow our caravan.

Circumstances change as one travels through life and as my children matured, married and flew the nest I told myself it was time to drive something a little more luxurious.

In fifty years of family motoring we had always bought British. Something to be proud of but I'm afraid that on the 19th May 1980 I was tempted to purchase from Rivervale of Pangbourne what I consider to be one of the finest cars in the world, the Mercedes-Benz 450 SLC Coupe. Not only was it almost new but by a remarkable coincidence the registration number ARH 450S reads Albert & Ruth Houghton. I excuse any suggestion of extravagance on my part in owning such a vehicle, after all, having driven around in either cheap or antiquated motor cars for almost half a century, it was time for something better.

The SLC Coupe is a superb car. My wife and I can now drive in effortless comfort. The car is an easily-handled power pack, when the car is cruising at seventy miles per hour the rev counter hovers around the 3500 mark which still leaves 3000 revs in reserve and one can take sharp corners as if the car is on rails.

Another point to remember is that at the end of the day it is satisfying to realise that one's vehicle is gaining in value as the years pass by, something that cannot be claimed for the majority of cars.

The fun starts here

Fully extended, our dining table at Mousefield is ten feet long and five feet wide. The highly polished solid mahogany top, which is two inches thick and supported on four massive carved legs, weighs almost half a ton so it doesn't get moved too often! Twelve people can sit and dine in comfort and there is no doubt it has seen many changes in the hundred years or so it has been around.

Breakfast at the farm was eaten in dribs and drabs in the kitchen. Late risers barely had time to swallow a bowl of cornflakes before rushing down the drive to catch the school bus. It was not unusual to see someone return, dragging their feet up the garden path. "Bus was early today mum, can you take me to school by car?" If this happened too often the best cure was to make the offender cycle!

With the exception of hay-time and the corn harvest, the main meal of the day was taken at six o'clock in the evening. The family seldom numbered less than nine. Mum, dad and seven children, invariably there were also one or two friends, friends of friends, or long-lost relatives to swell the number. My first wife Peggy enjoyed cooking for her large family and she was an excellent cook. On occasion I would turn my hand to the task, my speciality was jugged hare, a rare treat, when properly prepared and marinated in the refrigerator for at least 48 hours, perhaps one of the great dishes of the world! No-one had need to leave the table hungry in our house, but that doesn't mean that there was never a squabble over the last slice of apple tart when I served 'seconds'.

There was one occasion when a fight developed between Richard and Stephen over the possession of the tomato sauce bottle. With a whoop of delight the victor snatched the prize, but the top was loose with the result that the contents shot out and upwards on to the ceiling. All sauces were banned for some time after that.

With a large family one must have discipline and good organisation, especially at meal times if a 'free for all' is to be avoided. I always sat at the head of the table, my wife at the opposite end, the children all at their allotted place between. Older members fed younger ones, but it is surprising how quick a baby can feed him or herself if food is placed before them and hunger nags!

It was my job to carve the joint and dish out the pud, always serving clockwise. It is most important and quite an art to ensure fair shares for all. In our household there was an unwritten law that no-one started eating until grace was said and I had picked up my knife and fork.

A visit to the butcher's shop was rare indeed, practically all the meat we ate was home produced. Once a year a beef animal was slaughtered, jointed and frozen. The hide dried and tanned to be used as a mat by the fire – they never wear out and are still in use today after many years of service - three or four fat lambs and two porkers ended up the same way. We fattened capons the year round and turkeys at Christmas time. Being a useful shot the household was never short of rabbit, pigeon, duck or even the occasional Canada Goose, not to mention pheasants when in season. Hens provided eggs, the cows our daily milk, cream and butter. Our large fertile garden grew almost every vegetable, and vast quantities of spuds.

The orchard provided delicious apples, pears and plums, the fruit garden gave us strawberries, raspberries, loganberries, gooseberries, red, white and black currants. In season the meadows gave us mushrooms by the basketful. If that was not enough the blackberry, hazel, crab, sloe and bullace all yielded their treasures.

We made potent wine from dandelions, cowslips, rhubarb, parsnips, oak leaves and even tea leaves. We brewed beer and made elderflower champagne, a delicious drink but highly dangerous when fermenting, if the bottles are not strong enough. We learned this fact from bitter experience one year when the bottles started to explode, shattering glass and our prime champagne all over the utility room. The family were highly amused to see dad wearing his war time steel helmet and other protective clothing in order to remove the remaining unexploded bottles to a safe area of the garden!

If my family and I had lived in the Stone Age I suppose I would have been described as a good provider, the hunter returns laden so to speak. It always seemed that arriving home from some journey or even from a walk around my own farm, I returned with something edible.

Once each week I delivered heavy hogs to 'Harris of Calne'. At the rear of their bacon factory one could purchase 'damaged pies' at a fraction of shop prices. These pies were quite fresh, made that day but with the crust slightly burnt or broken, often the only damage was to the tinfoil containers. Damaged pie day was something the whole family looked forward to.

More journeys were made to 'Millers of Poole'. My lorry filled to capacity with two decks of fat pigs. This firm also had a small shop, hidden away up two flights of stairs at the rear of the factory. Here was sold best back bacon, black sausages, gammon steaks, cooked hams and damaged pies all at a discount on normal retail prices. I had been taking my pigs to this factory for some time before discovering the existence of this shop. When I did the assistant refused to serve me. "This shop is for staff only", she explained. Being a persistent so-and-so, I asked to speak to the manager. When he arrived on the scene I said, "I'm told this shop of yours only serves staff, well these pigs of mine I feed every day, clean them out, attend their every need, then transport them seventy miles from my farm in Berkshire. If I'm not staff I don't know who is! If it wasn't for chaps like me you would all be out or a job." He saw my point of view and from that day onwards I was considered 'on the staff'.

When the children were small I made a habit of returning from market every Thursday with a mixture of seven different chocolate bars, but distribution caused many arguments and frequent scraps so I took to buying seven all alike. This method also failed. I was greeted with complaints. "You've bought Mars Bars again dad, you know I don't like them". "Oh, not Fruit and Nut, we had those last week, remember?" or "No, not all Nugget Bars, I can't eat them, I've got loose teeth." In the end I got fed up, it just wasn't worth the trouble my generosity caused.

Long winter evenings, festive occasions especially at Christmas time brought fun and games, many of which were played around our dining table.

'Tippet' an hilarious party game for all age groups from five to ninety-five year olds. Never once can I remember any guest having heard of the game "Tippet, how do you play that?" they would ask. Simple to play, it generates endless fun, yet all one requires is a small coin or button plus the ability of every player to keep a poker straight face when challenged. Two captains are chosen who then select their team, ideally at least six players. The two teams now face each other sitting on either side of the table with their respective captains in the centre of each group.

The captain has the coin, he now calls, "Hands down", whereupon all his team's hands disappear under the table. First he moves his hands to the right, then to the left, passing the coin or pretending to. His team members pass the coin first one way, then the other or perhaps it doesn't get passed at all. It is all bluff and counter-bluff. Females giggle and squeal as knees get tickled or squeezed. If the coin gets dropped onto the floor that side is disqualified and it is passed to their opponents. At his discretion the captain calls 'up' whereupon all his team bring their clenched fists up and onto the table. The person who holds the coin tries desperately to hide his or her guilt with varied degrees of success.

One member of the opposing team has been chosen to discover who holds the coin. He or she is faced with twelve, fourteen or more hands in which the coin could be held. He points, saying at the same time "Take that hand away". This can be either one hand at a time or both hands of a player. By a simple process of elimination he reduces the number of clenched fists in front of him. If he thinks he knows who holds the coin he can call "Tippet" at any time.

If he guesses correctly the coin is passed to his side of the table. The team who holds the coin successfully twenty-one times is declared the winners. There are other versions of this game called crabs, creeps and bangs. Another game that caused endless fun and laughter was played with two decks of playing cards and one less walnut than the people in the game.

I often tell people that you don't have to purchase expensive games to keep children or adults amused at party times. One needs nothing more than a pack of playing cards, a two pence piece and a few walnuts.

Porky

Porky was a pet pig. By breeding a Large White, but he didn't live up to his name. He certainly wasn't large and often far from white! In fact he was a "darling", the runt of the litter. He had had a poor start in life, not only was he snubbed and bullied by his far larger brothers and sisters, but by the luck of the draw he had the least productive teat of the fourteen on his mother's pendulous udder, so poor was his milk supply that whilst his litter mates grew fatter and fatter he seemed to fade away.

He was just over two weeks old when I casually said over supper one evening, "I think I should knock that little squeaker pig on the head, he's never going to do us any good, he will eat as much food as the rest of the bunch when he grows up, that's if he ever does. He will never make me any money. I'll be out of pocket if I keep him, I reckon first loss will be best."

I had underestimated the emotional effect this brief statement would have on the younger members of my family sitting round the dining room table. A chorus of protests went up. "No, no dad, you mustn't do that, we love Porky, he's lovely, and he knows his name. My young son Richard spoke up. "I've got a good idea dad, lets wean him off his mum, we could give him some milk from Bobby's baby bottle, she don't need milk any more." "That's great," shouts another member of the family. "I bags feeding him." "Be quiet all of you, that's enough racket over a blooming pig," says I crossly.

"It was Richard's idea, if we wean 'im, he can feed 'im and don't forget that could be half-a-dozen times a day, and in the middle of the night too!! And don't poke your tongue out at Freddie like that Richard, just because you've won."

At the eleventh hour Porky had won a reprieve. He was installed in a chicken house with a large wire run in front, and a straw lined

"Porky at home, one of the family now"

dog basket for a bed. I had to admit, that despite his diminutive size he was quite a character. Two very intelligent bright eyes, the tiniest pink nose, two upright pixie-like ears and a very curly tail. He also had very sharp teeth and an ear-piercing squeal at feeding times.

On a more staple diet, Porky soon started to put on weight, I discovered that he was enjoying cornflakes and milk for breakfast, my tasty cheddar, and wholemeal bread for lunch and mashed potatoes with butter at supper time. He ate his straw bedding, chewed up the dog basket and rooted up the grass in his wire pen.

"Dad, I'm teaching Porky to do tricks," said one of the younger members of my family. "I shouldn't think there is any need for that" I replied. "He knows enough already."

The next thing, with a collar round his neck and a piece of binder twine attached he was being taken for walkies down the farm track!!

Farm life continued, winter turned to spring, spring to summer, Porky was still with us, one of the family now. His brothers and

"Porky at the Seaside"

sisters had long since made the one-way journey to the bacon factory.

When the children broke up from school my wife and I planned a short break between hay making and the corn harvest. We would tow our caravan to the New Forest, parking at a spot not too far from the sea.

Excitement grew as holiday time drew near. "What about Porky, dad, can he come on holiday too?" "Course not," I replied, "Whoever heard of a pig going to the seaside?" "Oh, why not dad? He's good now, he leads ever so well, he doesn't squeak any more, and he's house trained." I pointed out something that my family had forgotten. When the sun shines he sleeps in his pen, at the sea he will get sunburn, white pigs burn quickly in the sun and their ears curl up.

"We will put sun lotion on him dad and he can wear a hat with holes cut for his ears." "You will get him some dark glasses too, I expect," says I. With that I capitulated. Porky was to come on holiday with the family. At least he wouldn't need a spade, he was quite capable of digging up the entire beach at Mudeford with his snout!!

I was running a large car for a large family at the time, a shooting brake affair. Porky sat on an old blanket on the back seat, we hadn't gone but five miles when a shout from the rear announced, "Stop dad, I think Porky is going to be sick!" I quickly pulled into the side, there wasn't quite so much traffic on the A34 in those days. Our pet pig, still on a lead is walked on the grass verge, spends a penny, all is well once more. This time we get no more delays and within the hour camp is pitched in a quiet glade of the New Forest. If Porky decides to take a walk on his own in the woods it is certain he will be lost for ever. Well, I tell myself, that would solve one problem that had been on my mind for sometime. Porky couldn't live with us for ever and I couldn't for the life of me see my family eating him, so what the devil could we do with him, he was costing me a fortune to keep. Perhaps vegetarians have got a point there!

Oh well, we were all on holiday, we will cross that bridge when we get to it, I told myself.

Over the years we were to have many more pet pigs, latterly one in particular comes to mind.

Miss Potter's rise to fame was brought about by the simple fact that she became an unmarried mother at a very early age. Like her pig-sty companions she was destined for the bacon factory and that day was fast approaching when, one morning at feeding time, I noticed that she showed all the signs of being pregnant. But, I asked myself, how could that be? All the other pigs in the pen were either female or castrated males and she hadn't been out of the piggery on any visit to the stud boar. The secret came out when on close inspection I discovered that one of her male companions had somehow missed his appointment with the vet's scalpel!

Her indiscretion won her a last minute reprieve. The rounded curves of her backside were no longer going to end up as sweet cured Christmas hams, nor the rest of her carcass as pork pies and sausages.

In due course her litter mates were loaded into a livestock wagon on their one-way journey. Miss Potter was carefully moved to the farrowing unit where a close eye was kept on her condition. The fact that she was so young and immature could signify a difficult confinement.

She continued to swell, but of course I had no idea when to expect the happy event.

My grandchildren, Edward and Catherine, who were now living close by, paid a quick visit each morning before school to check all was well. There was great excitement early one morning. "Mummy, ring grandad quick, Miss Potter has got some babies." On receiving the message I left my half-eaten rasher and egg, drove the short distance down the rutted driveway which connects the two farms.

Two very excited youngsters ran to the garden gate to greet me, almost dragging me across the meadow to the farrowing house, Miss Potter was lying in a nest of straw giving little grunts of pleasure, it almost seemed as if she was talking to her offspring

"Miss Potter and Family"

55

Eight tiny white piglets had at that stage, only one aim in life, immediate access to the milk bar! The children felt that the happy event warranted a day off school. This was not to be, but they certainly wasted no time on their return to check all was well with the new family.

At three days old the piglets had their iron injection, this to prevent anaemia and a white scour, that affects young pigs kept in an unnatural environment. They also had their sharp front teeth nipped off to prevent damage to their mother's nipples.

Miss Potter turned out to be an excellent parent, taking great care of her brood. When the piglets were a month old I turned them and their mother outside on free-range. Each day the children on returning from school searched around the farm buildings to bring them in for the night. With each passing day the young pigs got more venturesome, exploring further and further afield. Their freedom ended when a telephone call from an irate neighbour informed me that a sow with a crowd of little pigs was in the process of rooting up his front lawn and wrecking his herbaceous border!

Miss Potter produced several more litters over the next few years. Every six months she "went off on her holidays". At least that is what the grandchildren were told. She must have had a grand time because on her return it wasn't many months later that another crowd of little potters came into the big wide world!!

The Story of the Water Butts

The year was 1958, our piggery or pig parlour as it was often referred to, was full to bursting point. In fact we should have been displaying a notice over the main entrance "No Vacancies". The reason, as always, was that pig prices were very low, suffering one of their traditional troughs of depression. My father and I couldn't resist buying what appeared to be such bargains. On the other hand feeding stuffs were most expensive. If we could reduce input costs on pig food and pork prices were to recover we could make a bomb. Although a regular reader of "Farmer's Weekly", I rarely gave the adverts a second glance, yet on this occasion I couldn't fail to miss a full page offering 'Milkiwey Concentrate' - a semi-solid Milk Extract rich in the valuable protein Lactalbumin. Whey products Ltd claimed 'Milkiwey could be included up to a level of 25% in trough-fed rations.' The price delivered to your farm was quoted at £27 per ton. It was supplied in free non-returnable wooden barrels with a net content of 5cwts each.

Initially I placed an order for two tons. Three days later a heavily laden lorry crept up the farm drive. "I would like those barrels of whey put into the stock-feed store please" I tell the driver. "Can't do that mate, I can only roll 'em off the back. Wants a soft patch of ground too, or they'll burst open and you'll have one hell of a mess." A metal skid was placed on the rear of the lorry, down which slid the heavy barrels to land with a thud on the grass. The driver did kindly assist me in standing them upright, where they stood like soldiers on parade. Made of hardwood the barrels were tightly sealed and could only be opened by smashing the top with an axe.

From then onwards our pigs thrived, their coats shone, their tails curled and they put on weight as never before. During the next decade the pig unit made money, the only snag was that acres of our best farmland was slowly going out of production, vanishing under the cover of massive wooden kegs!

A solution to the problem just had to be found. Ever on the lookout for a means to raise more much needed cash, I placed a small advertisement in our local paper. "For Sale, Strong Wooden Kegs £1 each delivered to your door. Suitable for water butts or as garden furniture." Pounds came rolling in.

I'll never forget one particular incident. An order for two of my water butts came from a titled lady living over the border in nearby Hampshire. Mrs Day, my late mother-in-law had sold her house in Tilehurst on the death of her husband and had taken up residence at Mousefield. She loved nothing better than to accompany me on country trips in the cattle lorry and it was unusual if we didn't return with some laughable incident to report to the family over supper.

On this occasion we chugged along through the beautiful wooded countryside south of Newbury before slowly climbing the chalk hills of Watership Down, then through a pair of magnificent wrought iron gates, finally down a gravel drive flanked by well manicured lawns.

I drew up at the imposing front door. My mother-in-law was highly amused. "Goodness me, this is a bit grand Bert, you sure we are at the right place?" she asked. I got out of the cab, marched boldly to the door and pulled on a handle attached to a long chain. A bell rang in the secluded depth, heavy footsteps sounded in the hall as someone approached. The door opened, there stood the butler. A tall, severe looking man with a haughty expression on his face. He looked me up and down and something told me he strongly disapproved of my lorry parked outside the main entrance. "Yes, what do you want?" He enquired rather crossly. "Two barrels for her Ladyship", I boldy announced. For a few seconds this statement seemed to catch him off guard, then his solemn features softened and he actually smiled. "Two barrels for her Ladyship" he repeated with some surprise in his voice. "Well, I've often wished to give the old so and so one barrel but never two!" He immediately realised his indiscretion, the smile vanished as quickly as it came. "What exactly do you mean Sir?" "They are two water butts really, she ordered 'em on the telephone, s'pose she wants to catch rainwater in them to water the roses and things" I explained. "Anyway where shall I put them?" "Not out here that's for sure, you should have gone to the tradesman's entrance with a vehicle like that. Wait there I will go and enquire." He turned and disappeared down the long carpeted hall. On his return a few minutes later, he pointed to a small doorway in a high brick wall, obviously the entrance to the vegetable garden. "Would you please unload your goods by that door then come back here, her Ladyship would like to meet you and would you care to partake in afternoon tea?" "Yes, thank you very much but what about my mother-in-law, she is waiting in the cab?" I said. "Bring her along too, I'm sure that will be in order." I clambered into the driving seat, started the engine, drove the short distance to the garden door, dropped the tailboard and unloaded, "We are going into the big house for tea mother, how 'bout that?" "What! you're joking surely, anyway I'm not dressed proper" she replied. "Course you are, you'll do, you look quite smart" I said, holding open the cab door and helping her down from the passenger seat.

The mistress of the house was not the dragon painted by the butler, she was a genteel, well-spoken Victorian lady who explained that since losing her dear husband some years ago she met few people, many of her friends and relatives had passed on. My new friend, the butler, poured tea into elegant china cups. "Sugar and milk Madam, and what about you Sir?" he enquired, in his most cultured voice. My late mother-in-law was a charming person who always got along fine with everyone, soon the two ladies were chatting away like life-long friends. I was plied with questions about my farm, how many cows I milked, did I have sheep, what crops I grew, what about children and how in the world did I come by all those wooden butts? "Do you drink a lot of beer?" she asked with a laugh.

A very pleasant hour was spent in this charming lady's company, after such a lovely tea I felt rather guilty pocketing two new pound notes when the time came to depart!

Ponies & Hunters

Living on a farm with a family of seven children it was not to be unexpected that over the years we had a varied succession of ponies, Michael, my eldest son never had any inclination to get in the saddle, that is not to say he never rode a horse, just that he never pestered me with the usual request "I'd like a pony dad".

Ponies were not difficult to find. One only had to drop a hint at the local market that you were on the look-out for a quiet ride and it was not long before the phone rang with some character offering you a bargain.

His son or daughter had unfortunately outgrown their present mount, which of course was absolutely sound in wind and limb, very quiet, good over jumps and provided it went to a good home the price was not important. One didn't enquire how many ponies his child had outgrown in the past!! I have never been a 'horsey man' and therefore lay no claim to being an expert on the subject, but I did know that when purchasing horse flesh one had to be very, very careful indeed. There are of course honest traders but also many horse dealers that know more tricks than the proverbial monkey!

One can of course have the animal vetted but when buying a quiet, reasonable priced child's pony I preferred to back my own opinion and perhaps more by way of luck than judgement we did manage to get some very spirited steeds.

A few still retain a place in my memory, Chocolate Lady, of pure Welsh Mountain blood was a flea-bitten grey, oddly enough, not grey at all but really dirty white with brown spots. She was purchased from a farm on the borders of Exmoor. Although quiet and well broken she enjoyed her freedom and was sometimes difficult to catch. Once haltered and saddled any of the children could safely ride her. Two years later we had her covered with the

Chocolate lady and Flash

result that her offspring 'Flash' was our first success in horse breeding. Son Tim laid claim to the new arrival and had the halter on its head from day one, 'Flash' so named because of the conspicuous white blaze on its forehead was always Tim's pony. He walked it round the farm, lunged it in the meadow and had it saddle broke at two years old.

Rupert, a grey gelding was also of Welsh Mountain stock. He was truly wild, completely mad at times. One day we rounded him up, got him into a tight corner of the cow yard, and got reins and bridle over his head with great difficulty. Bareback, fearless Tim took off across the field, but Rupert knew some tricks. He headed full gallop for the boundary fence and at the last second he swerved without warning. If you were still on his back, he'd buck high in the air as well as any Wild West bronc, Tim was thrown many times but tamed this fiery little 13.2 eventually.

'Pepy' was his name, a brown Shetland, standing only three feet high at the shoulder. I purchased this pathetic little creature for two reasons, one was that our youngest at the time was complaining bitterly that he was the only member of the family without a mount and two, because I just felt so sad for the poor animal. He did look a sorry sight, confined to a tiny orchard, he'd been half starved, ill treated and what made him appear really odd was that he had no mane. His only companion had been a huge white billy goat and it was the goat who was responsible for Pepy's bald appearance, having eaten the pony's mane and half of its tail!! I purchased the two for £40. I must have been naive because I turned the goat out with the dairy cows believing at that time in the 'Old Wives Tale' that a goat on the farm prevented one's herd from Foot and Mouth disease. We did of course keep the goat well away from the ponies. It certainly had some odd eating habits. Richard used to feed him on paper bags which seemed to be its favourite meal, Billy the goat didn't sojourn long at Mousefield. He was found dead one morning, we had him opened up by the vet whose verdict was that he had died from a blocked intestine. From what Billy had been eating this was no great surprise!

Buying your pony is only the start of what eventually turns out to be a very expensive business. When one recovers from the pleasure of being showered with thanks, hugs and kisses from an enraptured daughter it dawns on you that one cannot do much with a pony without equipment.

My children must have thought that money really did grow on trees! With a new pony in the home paddock Saturday morning meant an early visit to the tack shop. "Got your cheque book dad?" Enquires my jubilant son or daughter as we set off in my antiquated motor vehicle which should have gone to the scrap yard years before if I hadn't spent so much money on four-legged horse power.

A good leather saddle is an expensive item but one mustn't skimp on price. Its got to be a comfortable fit for both pony and rider. One would always blame oneself if your offspring fell breaking bones or worse, all due to an illfitting saddle. Bridle, switch, brushes, comb, knee pads and a New Zealand rug are just a part of your pony's accessories. If it spent the greater part of the day in a loose box, pony nuts, bedding straw and our best cow hay vanished at an alarming rate. Every two or three months I would be asked to get the farrier over quickly. "You know there is the gymkhana next Saturday dad and now Myra has cast a shoe." All farm work and problems are shelved, an urgent telephone call is made. "I'm sorry Mr Pirquet is very busy" says his wife, "I'll put you down for a visit in a fortnights time, that is the best I can do." "No please, please, I plead, he must come tomorrow or the next day. The pony is jumping this coming Saturday, I will pay him cash on the day if that helps." Money talks, catastrophe is averted yet again.

Expenditure hasn't stopped yet, there is still the rider to fit out. Jodhpurs, black high leather riding boots, habit, pony club tie and of course, the best in safety hats.

The next request is for riding lessons. "You know you can't ride well enough to teach me dad" I am told quite truthfully. There is no shortage of excellent riding schools around the district, some of my children had lessons at my cousin Phil Povey's farm near Kingsclere, others with John Mills at Curridge. Bobby my youngest daughter showed most promise in the equestrian stakes. She quickly outgrew her thirteen hand pony Myra. In 1979 I purchased Folly a 15.2 hunter, ten years old at that time. This particular acquisition sent my overdraft soaring upwards by twelve hundred pounds and a made-to-measure leather saddle by a further three hundred. Local building contractor Sammy Hughes erected a very useful stable and tack room for the sum of two thousand pounds. Some said "You're spoiling that daughter of yours" and no doubt they had a point, but

"The Author's first horse"

others told me that horses "filled the gap between toys and boys" in teenage girls lives. Folly was like a well-tuned racing car in those days. She would react to the touch of your knee or stirrup and respond to the slightest twitch on the rein but she possessed a strong will which required strict discipline to keep under control but once she sensed you were boss she was an angel.

It was Bobby who needed schooling not the horse! She took advanced riding lessons at Miss Tufnal's, spending many of her school holidays at this establishment, living in and working at the stables.

In her time Folly won rosettes by the dozen in local gymkhanas and cross country events. More often than not we returned home in jubilation but there were black days too when my juvenile daughter shed tears of frustration. "Why did my stupid horse have to refuse at the last fence? She hadn't put a foot wrong all day, then in the jump off against the clock she lets me down. I was in line for the cup too."

Folly is still with us in 1990 but living in well-earned retirement now that my daughter has married and emigrated to Australia.

I apologise if it appears that I am complaining of time and money spent, it was all in a good cause and I would love to have it all over again.

The days work finished, I'd sit in the garden on an early summer night with a pint of beer in my hand, and watch my children putting their ponies over a few jumps, made from painted poles resting on some old oil drums, whilst behind me the great orange moon crept slowly behind the oak trees of Mousefield copse, gaining to brilliant silver as it rose high to illuminate the moth-filled garden.

All the family and myself had great fun from the long list of horses, ponies and donkeys that shared our lives.

Clive and the donkeys

Over the years frequent visits were made at weekends to "Uncle Bob's Farm": The late Mr Robert Sheerman and my mother's sister, Aunt Glady, lived and farmed at Ivory Farm, Burghclere, which nestles peacefully at the foot of Beacon Hill. The main attraction for the children was that Uncle Bob kept two donkeys. The largest of the pair, a gelding was a strong well built animal, and if in the right mood capable of quite a burst of speed over a short distance.

"Come on Bert, you are always boasting how you rode to hounds in your youth, jump on and have a ride, show us what you can do," implored my uncle. "Yes, go on dad its great fun" chorused the kids. Big Ned as he was called, stood quite still as I clambered on his back. Clutching the reins I gave my mount a good thump in the ribs with the heels of my boots, at the same time someone behind gave it a sound whack on its backside. We took off in top gear, full gallop across the meadow. I remember gritting my teeth as I clung on for dear life, knowing full well that if I fell off I'd be the laughing stock of the cheering onlookers in the rear. What I didn't know was that Big Ned was trained to stop on command. A loud "whoa there" from Uncle Bob caused a classic emergency stop. I shot over its head landing in a very undignified manner into a freshly dropped cow pat!! My audience were clapping their hands in glee and bursting their sides with laughter. "Well done dad, I knew you were a good rider" shouted one of my kids. My steed had bolted to the far side of the field taking no more interest in the proceedings. Creeping back, stiff, bruised and rather smelly, Uncle Bob said, "Never mind Bert all the best riders have to fall off at least once in their life!"

Homeward bound after the 'Donkey Derby' my wife and children were in high spirits. "You going to buy me a donkey dad?" enquired my son Tony. "I whons a nonkey too," Baby Jane chirps in. "No I'm

Down to earth

not, we have got two ponies at home now, I'm definitely not spending my money on long-eared asses, especially after this afternoon's episode, I consider they are dangerous, untrustworthy animals," "Course they're not dad, you've got it all wrong, none of us fell off remember?"

The weekend over, back to work, back to school, the subject was taboo, hopefully it had died a natural death. Market day a few weeks later one of my farmer acquaintances in the course of conversation said, "I 'ears you be on the look-out for a good donkey?" "No I ain't, who ever told you that story," I replied with some surprise. "Oh, word gets round you know, t'was ole Bob Sheerman over Burghclere way, told me as 'ow you'd bin over his place trying to buy one o-his but he wouldn't sell. Said som'at 'bout you rode one of 'em but it proved too much for you." I noticed that my friend had a sly grin on his face but I thought it prudent to keep quiet. "Well, if you wants a donkey get in touch with Nick Perry. He has got quite a few grazing on Basingstoke Common. Give him a ring, he'll fix you up."

Back home again I said nothing of the day's conversation, but I did ring Mr. Perry. "Yes, pleased to show you round," he replied. I could have any one I wished for £25. A date and time was agreed. I really must be crackers I told myself. A few days later, morning milking finished, stock fed and the children gone off to school, with a wad of five pound notes in my pocket I set forth on my secret mission in my Austin cattle truck. In the 1960's, Basingstoke Common had not been developed, it was a pleasant secluded area with scrub bushes and very poor grass land on which certain local farmers had the right to graze their stock.

I met Mr. Perry at the agreed spot, parked the lorry then we walked out across the common together. Plain nurse cows with calves at foot nibbled away at the thin pasture. Watching our progress from the brow of the hill was a group of eight long-eared donkeys, large ones, small ones, some grey in colour, some brown, one a piebald.

"I want a quiet one that any of my young children can ride and is not too difficult to catch". All on 'em be saddle and bridle broke you, kids come out from the town, jump on and ride 'em bare back" said Nick. He was quite right, they were quiet. Problem was I just didn't know which one to choose.

I was really taken aback when suddenly Nick said, "Buy the lot you, save the bother of picking one out, your kids can sort the one they want, then you can sell the rest for a profit, plenty of people want donkeys for their children these days. To tell you the truth, I'm fed up with the damn things, take the whole bunch you can have 'em for £20 each."

Not giving much thought of what trouble I could be letting myself in for I rather rashly said, "I've got a hundred pounds in cash for the lot, take them now if we can get them loaded. £140 in crisp new fivers was to clinch the deal.

Homeward bound with my latest purchase I couldn't make up my mind who was the biggest donkey, one of those in the rear or the one in the cab!! Back at the farm I received a mixed reception, the children were in ecstasy, Dora apprehensive, my wife Peggy was furious, saying "Whatever are we going to do with that lot, they'll eat all the cow grass and wake everybody at dawn with their he-haws, why couldn't you have been sensible and bought just one?" When we turned them loose in the home paddock with the two ponies they danced round in circles, kicked up their hind legs, bared their teeth, and promptly chased our two startled ponies round and round the meadow. What a shambles we had for a while.

That weekend my children and all their friends for miles around had the time of their lives. They caught them, fed them bread, biscuits, carrots, apples and goodness knows what. Rode them with and without saddles or bridles, fell off umpteen times and in general had a smashing time, but such novelty soon wears off. I just had to find a buyer.

My saviour, Clive Povey, a second cousin of mine was in business as a farmer and cattle dealer, the last person one would expect to purchase my long eared friends.

I retained the two favourites which we had around the farm for many years, the other six I sold to Clive for £25 each. He was to take a lot of ribbing from his farming friends in the next few weeks.

Clive and the donkeys became a standing joke.

Dora

No book of mine would be complete without a chapter on Dora.

In 1948, long before milk quotas were thought of in this country, in common with most other dairy farmers my cow numbers were increasing, which in turn meant more calves to rear, more mouths to feed, more bedding down, more wheelbarrow loads of muck to shift. The endless daily chores were getting my wife and I down. We reasoned that we could afford to pay for another pair of hands, but our need was for a willing, conscientious person competent in milking cows by hand. The fact that at that time we had no farm cottage accommodation greatly restricted our choice of workman.

Placing a small advertisement in our local paper for a cowman - under the sex discrimination law of today one would use the word cowperson - we had replies from a motley collection of hopefuls, from fourteen year old school leavers to a fifty year old bus driver who cherished a lifelong ambition to work with animals, previously his only experience with livestock was the fact that as a young lad he had cleaned out pigstys on his uncle's farm at weekends and school holidays!

I had given no thought to the possibility of employing a woman but a few days after the paper had been published, I was working in the yard when I noticed a lady approaching on a bicycle.

Miss Dora Jerome was applying for the herdsman's job advertised in the Newbury Weekly News on Thursday last. She explained that currently she was working at the Swift Cleaners in town, but wished to get back into farming. To my enquiries she replied that she was a farmer's daughter, her parents had had a small holding at Combe Bissett near Salisbury. At the outbreak of the Second World War she had joined the Women's Land Army serving for six years, working for the whole period as dairymaid for Mr & Mrs Gathorne-Hardy at Donnington Priory. She had been in complete charge of their small herd of Pedigree Guernsey Cows. Hand milking them twice each day and rearing the heifer calves to maturity.

She expressed no qualms about cycling out to the farm each day for the six a.m. milking, come rain or shine, ice or snow, in daylight and in darkness. Quite a journey from her lodgings in Monk's Lane on the other side of town.

That was how Dora came to Mousefield and as time passed she became almost part of our family. For the next thirty-seven years she conscientiously milked our cows, reared the baby calves, fed the pigs, shut up the poultry, collected the eggs and if necessary, took charge of other animals, which occasionally I brought home from my travels, such as ponies, donkeys, goats, sheep and tame rabbits. There were even times when she took charge of our ever-increasing stock of children, but always fought shy of nappy changing.

After a while Dora moved, renting a flat in the old Chapel run by the YWCA behind Camp Hopson's shop. Eventually the building was demolished to make way for a car park. This was to prove a blessing in disguise for our 'cowgirl'.

Ever since Dora had received notice to quit she had been worried about her future. "I dunno what I'm going to do, I'd like to still work 'ere cos' I likes the cows and calves and things but I just got no place to live, and its a long old bike ride backwards and forwards everyday from town even if I could find another place to rent."

For days I had given much thought to the problem. Peggy and I had come to rely on our new assistant but with our growing family there was no room in the farmhouse.

On the north side of the house was the milk dairy, adjoining was a small room 6ft by 12ft with just one window and a door. It had no particular role in the farm set up being used simply to store all kinds of junk and the usual strange bits and pieces that us farmers tend to keep in the belief that one day they may be needed.

We were in the dairy one morning tying labels on the milk churns and wheeling them out to load on the waiting horse-cart when I said, "How 'bout moving into the store room next door Dora? We will clear it out, get a bed, an electric cooker, put up some curtains find a chair or two, you'd be fine in there for the time being." She replied with some misgivings. "'Spose I could but there is hardly room to swing a cat in there and sides, where you going to put all that ole rubbish, best have a good bonfire I reckon."

The room was cleared scrubbed clean and redecorated to Dora's colour scheme, the necessary furniture and cooking appliances installed.

"What about a toilet?" says Dora, "Thats a good question, I hadn't thought of that." I replied, "As you know we've only got one in the house and with seven in the family we don't want to lengthen the queue at busy times, the seat never gets cold as it is!! "'Bout if I built a tin hut in the wood and placed an Elsan in it, that would do the trick Dora, wouldn't it"? "'Spose it will have to", she said. "Going to be darn cold in the winter though traipsing up there amongst the trees in the dark." "Oh, don't moan so Dora, there is usually a solution to every problem, take a torch and don't sit up there too long" was my answer to that one.

Up went the little hut, three foot square and six feet high, camouflaged in green paint and well hidden by a dense cover of blackthorns. A winding path led to the door with the one word 'Private' written boldly in red. Give us a shout when the bucket's full Dora, I'll do the necessary."

Talk about living over the shop! For the next twelve years poor Dora lived next door to the dairy and quite honestly she didn't have room to swing a cat but that didn't prevent her having half-a-dozen cats waiting on the doorstep every morning for their daily ration of fresh milk. I was often shocked to see such large containers filled to the brim. "If you are as generous as that Dora I'm not going to have any milk to send off to the creamery, I counted ten cats there this morning, we will soon have all the strays in the neighbourhood calling for free board and lodgings." "Ah! well, its an ill wind that never blows anyone any good", as they say: no rat or mouse managed to survive long on our farm despite its name!

Dora loved her calves, within a few days of birth she would give them names often applicable to their colouring or individuality. Baby calves, like children are all different and quickly develop a unique character. Taking over a new charge, usually at three days old, Dora often took me to book. "Don't look to me like you have squirted that purple stuff on his belly, if it gets infection through its navel and dies you'll blame me." "I was busy Dora, got forgotten, it will be alright, keep them well bedded down, there is plenty of clean wheat straw in the barn", I replied with my usual optimism.

Dora with another safe delivery

Returning from a weekend off duty, come Monday morning Dora closely scrutinized her calves. If she found any to be sick or off colour the whole world knew about it. She'd storm round the buildings until she found me. As soon as I saw her coming I knew there was trouble. "Who fed the calves this weekend I'd like to know". Whoever it was gave them too much milk or didn't mix it right, they be scouring their heads off. Somebody will have to go down to the vet and get some 'dollup'. In Dora's vocabulary all medication was referred to under the general term 'dollup' "Alright Dora, keep calm. It was the new boy I've just taken on who fed at the weekend, next time you have time off I'll feed the calves myself."

Dora turned and made off muttering something like. "Gow'in to take me all wick to get 'em right, 'alt to have more sense letting that boy feed, he don't know their 'eads from their backsides."

One calf in particular comes to mind. Tom Thumb, so named because he was so tiny. Born two months prematurely his chances of survival were slim. Unlike a human baby he couldn't be placed in an oxygen tent, attached by wires and tapes and monitored twenty-four hours each day by devoted nurses. He was too small and weak to suckle his mother, for one thing he couldn't reach her teats! With colustrum from his own dam Dora fed him every four hours, night and day, using one of our baby bottles that was out of commission at the time.

There were many days when we didn't think he was going to make it but Tom Thumb clung to life with great tenacity. By the time he should have been born he was the size of a normal full-time calf. For the next fourteen months Dora fed him on the best hay, the most expensive rearing nuts, he never lowered himself to eating grass in the meadow. Lead on a halter every day he was exercised, brushed and groomed with lavish care.

Unfortunately he put on weight so rapidly he outgrew his strength with the result that his knee joints gave way. When one is farming for a living one hard lesson one must learn is not to make pets or develop too deep an affection for any particular animal.

Tom Thumb could hardly walk, he was fat and overweight. Dora had a few days holiday to come, as usual she had booked a coach trip to some distant corner of the British Isles. When she returned Tom Thumb had gone. The following weekend quite a substantial number of Newbury residents enjoyed succulent steaks for Sunday lunch!

Another unforgettable calf born and reared at Mousefield was 'Bellboy' one of my first full Pedigree Dairy Shorthorns. By the time he was four years old and fully grown, he was huge yet so placid one could sit astride his flat, broad back as he slowly plodded his way to pasture. For many years monarch of the dairy herd yet he had to earn his living like the rest of us! When his time came to abdicate to a younger animal he was taken by cattle wagon to Newbury Market. Going over the weighbridge the scales recorded over one ton, twice the weight of a normal size cow. I lead him round the sale ring on the end of a bull-stick clipped to a big brass ring through his nostril.

"What am I bid for this fine bull gentlemen" said the auctioneer Fred Cole in his usual gabble. "I'm told he's still a stockgetter if any of you are interested in breeding from him." "I got fifty quid sir, I'm more interested in how many steaks I can get out of him than calves" shouted some wag. The auctioneer's gavel came down at £130, certainly by far the highest price I had ever received for a farm animal to date.

Over the years my farm increased in size. By 1960 we were farming some 300 acres. Brothers, Alec and Roy Adnams worked on our farms from the time they left school. We still lacked decent accommodation. Roy, now married, lived in a caravan with his wife who was expecting. I applied and was granted planning permission for a farm bungalow. In the construction work professional assistance was given by my late Uncle, Douglas Houghton who had been in the building trade most of his life, otherwise Roy and myself did all the basic work, digging out the footings by pick and shovel, getting the levels and laying concrete foundations. All the bricks were salvaged from an old wall at Red Farm. Dismantled, stacked, cleaned and transported to site mostly by the labour of my wife and our own children. They all worked like slaves. We tackled all the decorating inside and out, eventually, two years later, this tied cottage was ready to receive our first workman.

"What you going to do with your caravan Roy?" I enquired. "Dunno really unless old Dora would like to buy it, be much better for her than cramped up there in that little box room", he replied. Dora purchased it for the sum of £120. That doesn't sound a very large figure today but in those days with farm wages set at £5 per week it represented six months solid saving. For the next twenty years Dora lived with her cats in the blue painted caravan parked under a massive evergreen holm oak tree by the side of our farmhouse. She cultivated a pretty rose garden and had a small lawn to sit out on summer evenings from where she could survey the wide expanse of our beautiful tranquil valley. If anything was amiss it didn't escape Dora's eye.

Each day she rose at dawn, and long before in winter, milked the cows, fed the calves, cleaned out the pigs. Other tasks were undertaken with skilled ability and one was to single and flat hoe our kale, swedes and mangel crops. Season followed season, the midday heat of summer found Dora following the baler strenuously stacking hay bales. "Don't screw that blessed baler down so tight, these darn bales must weigh best part of a ton each" she shouted at me above the roar of the tractor, as I lapped her once more.

There was one farm job that she failed completely. We had had a very wet, cold spring, field work was way behind schedule. "Dora, I can't afford to have you messing about cutting a few stinging nettles round the vegetable garden with your sickle. Could you not learn to drive the tractor between milking times?" It would be a great help if you could, just easy jobs, like harrowing the grass or a bit of rolling." "I'll have a go but you'll have to start the thing up" she replied. Next day after morning chores were completed Teddy, the standard Fordson with the flat roller hitched behind, was fuelled and ready to go. "I'll do a turn with you Dora whilst you get the hang of things. Now all you got to do is put your foot on the clutch, put it into gear, let your foot off slowly and I mean slowly or else he'll buck, then steer across the field in a straight line, nothing to it! "Alright for you to tell me all that, you bin driving tractors for years" says Dora. "Where's the brake, I wants to know how to stop the blessed thing." We steer an erratic course around the field. "You are doing well Dora, I'll leave you now, pack up at dinner time, that will do for today." Returning to the farmhouse I added a spot of whisky to my coffee. I was sweating and my knees were all of a shake. "Dora is driving the tractor, rolling the fourteen acres" I told my wife. "Well you know best I suppose but in my opinion she is safer and more at home on a milking stool" replies Peggy. A few minutes later there came frantic calls from two of the children playing in the farm yard, "Come quick dad, Dora has driven the tractor into the hay rick." Luckily the tractor had stalled. Our learner driver had dismounted, she was white as a sheet and almost in tears. "I was looking behind at the roller and when I looked round, there it was in front of me, I'd forgotten how to put the brake on and I just couldn't miss the darn thing." "Never mind, can't be helped Dora, at least the rick or tractor didn't catch fire."

So ended Dora's one and only attempt at tractor driving.

Today Dora lives in gracious retirement at No 8 Abberbury Close, Donnington. She missed the presentation of a long service medal by three short years but if any farm person deserved a decoration it was our Dora.

Dedication to the Dairy Cow

The point of this anecdote is to emphasize the inevitable consequence of 'progress'.

Three generations of our family have been milking cows for a living nigh on a hundred years. Rising at the crack of dawn, three hundred and sixty five days each year, with an extra day thrown in for
good measure each Leap Year! Twice each day rain or shine, snow
or blow with not even a break on Christmas Day.

Cows played an important role in my childhood on our small-
holding in Berkshire. On summer afternoons I'd hurry home from
school to call the cows in from the meadow for the second milking
of the day. This was the one thing I was quite good at. Most cowman walk around the field and with the aid of a dog or two, drive
them into the farmyard. I prided myself that I could stand by the
gate and with a 'come on', 'come on' they would start moving
towards me. Another of my jobs was to go down the row of cows,
whilst they tucked into their feed rations, and tie the chain around
their necks. Cows had horns in those days and a passing fly might
cause a cow to swing her head round giving the unwary a nasty poke
in the ribs!

The next job was to prepare them for milking by washing their
udders. Being hit on the head, or worse still across the eyes by a
swishing tail was another minor hazard. I loved those cows, I still
remember their sweet, warm breath, their soft warm flanks and their
great big eyes with eye lashes well over an inch in length.

My father started our dairy unit on his return from farming on the
prairies of Canada before the First World War. Milk was produced
and delivered to the doors of country cottages, schools, pubs, and
the gentry, by horsedrawn float, dipped out of a seventeen gallon
brass decorated churn by a pint or quart measure. Surplus produc-

tion was sold as butter or cheese made by my mother.

Hand milking is a slow, laborious and far from hygienic method of producing fresh milk. There were however certain compensations for the small herd, one's cows received far more individual attention, they all had names instead of a brand number, we knew from memory each animal's parentage and didn't have to touch a computer key to find out if and when a certain cow was due to calve. Life moved at a much more leisurely pace, there were not the pressures of recent years to produce more and yet more milk from an ever-increasing herd.

The cows generally lasted through more lactations, in fact most herds contained at least one matriarch with enough rings on her crumpled horns to denote a lifetime of twenty years or more around the yard. (A cow adds one more ring to its horns each year like a tree which also shows a growth ring each year), with perhaps three or four generations following in her footsteps, all with the same high-yielding, high butterfat performance of their great grandma. My father always had a few of these old favourites, boasting of their fantastic milk production to his neighbours and friends. Quoting with some exaggeration so many pounds weight of milk in the last lactation conveniently forgetting that it was often over two years since some of those old dears had last produced a calf. "Yes and 'er still gives over half-a-gallon a day you know", he would proudly add. For reasons explained in my first book, my father had moved to Dymond Farm, just north of Newbury. The agricultural depression of the early 1930's found him milking about a dozen mainly Shorthorn Crosses.

The formation of the Milk Marketing Board in 1933 gave dairy farmers a guaranteed market for the first time and farmers were relieved of their obligation to find their own milk buyer. The newly formed Board purchased all that we could produce at a price subject only to season and area adjustments. This heaven-sent opportunity allowed and indeed encouraged most dairy farmers to begin expanding their herds, which eventually, many years later led to massive overproduction, the butter mountain, the near bankruptcy of the E.E.C. and then finally, the restraint of the milk quota scheme in 1984,

Dad gave up the daily grind of delivering milk in bottles to the doorstep. Now he drove the horse and float to Newbury Station catching the milk train to London each morning. I guess that in about 1936 the Board commenced milk collection in our area. My father, considering himself something of a carpenter, built a wooden stand at the bottom of our farm track. Our daily production of two or three ten gallon churns of milk was taken away by lorry each day. The driver leaving an equal number of clean, empty churns on the stand. Motor traffic was increasing in speed and numbers and the transfer of full churns from the horse-drawn milk float to the stand became increasingly hazardous. One day a car being driven too fast, crashed into the rear of the milk float catapaulting dad over the side, head first into the roadside ditch. Luckily he made a soft landing but the horse bolted and was halfway to town before someone bravely managed to stop it! Following this episode another stand was constructed further up our farm drive adjacent to the cowshed. Now the driver could transfer the full churns in safety.

Taking over the tenancy of Mousefield Farm in 1946 with the small herd of Guernsey Cows, we milked two dairy herds for some years - my fathers mixed bag of Shorthorn Crosses and the Guernsey herd. All by hand of course! In 1948 it was decided to farm both farms as one unit. My father and I created a partnership trading as "F Houghton & Son" at the same time moving his cows to Mousefield. Over the next few years we gradually phased the Guernseys out and at the same time built up the cow numbers to thirty-two. In the brick built cowshed at Mousefield there was room to tie up sixteen, all in line at the feed manger, each cow secured by a chain fastened around its neck. Home grown fodder of hay, crushed barley, oats and chopped mangels were fed according to season at milking time.

Our first venture in mechanisation of the daily milking chore was by way of a 'Manus' two unit bucket plant. News soon spread around, "That them Houghtons up at Mousefield were about buying one of those new-fangled milking machines". In town next market day some of our more pessimistic farming friends issued dire warnings of the possible consequence of this rash investment. "Yer cows will get a lot of mastitis you know, on top oh that them machines are expensive to run, always wanting new liners and things. And after milking you will have to spend as long again washing the whole darn outfit, and don't forget you still got to strip 'um out after you remove the clusters. Nowt gwon'na beat a good pair of

hands with their owners ass squat firmly on a three-legged stool."
We chose to ignore this well intended advice.

I built a wooden shed on the north side of our cowshed to house
a small petrol driven motor, which incidentally, often refused to start
on frosty mornings! The two milking units worked by vacuum reg-
ulated by a pulsator on each lid. We tapped into the overhead line
with a long rubber tube set between each pair of cows. (The same
method is still shown in use on the Emmerdale Farm programme.)
Warm frothy milk was transferred into two smaller pails which were
carried by yoke through the garden to the dairy at the rear of the
farm house, here it was lifted some six feet into a vat, from there it
trickled slowly over the cooler, through a strainer and into the churn
placed beneath. Cold water circulated continuously through the
inside of the cooler but in the heat of summer it was difficult to cool
the milk enough, with the result that many full churns of sour milk
were returned to us the following morning. Our pigs lived well but
there isn't much fun getting the last drop of milk from one's cows
only to have it returned by the purchaser. Neither is it good for one's
bank balance!

Newly married and fired by the ambition of youth, my wife and I
decided we had nothing to lose and possibly much to gain by grading up our best Shorthorn cows. Previously my father had been running a 'flying herd', which meant that if he was in the local market
and milk cows were going cheap that day, he couldn't help but to
purchase two or three. The result being that there was a continuous
turnover of cows.

I tactfully explained to my father that this practice would have to
stop. We would breed our own replacements aiming for better
yields, higher butterfat and eventually have well bred pedigree stock
to dispose of.

The first step was to join the Shorthorn Society. I became a life
member. Next we presented a selection of our best shorthorn types
for 'grading up'. A well known judge of the breed came by appointment to inspect. The cows in question had to be true to type, with
good conformation, well shaped udders and begot by a pedigree
dairy Shorthorn bull. Those accepted were then registered as foundation animals in the Society Herd Book. Next step was to purchase
from W Cumber and Sons, Barncroft Farm, Theale, a young dark
roan stock bull.

This step-by-step road to full pedigree stock is a lifetime's work and only for the young man, not only does one's herd gain in value but one gets far more job satisfaction from the process. It was about this time in my career that we went T.T. The herd was tested for tuberculosis over a period of three days by a Ministry Vet. Two cows failed the test and were immediately sent for slaughter, another classified doubtful, resulted in a re-test for this animal six weeks later. She passed, saved from the chop by a minute measurement of the calliper.

Thus was born "Mousefield Attested Pedigree Dairy Shorthorns". It did mean a lot of extra paper work. Keeping the register, milk yields, butterfat, ear-numbers and the necessity to register each new-born calf before it was one month old, but my wife accepted the challenge.

The breeding of Mousefield Bellboy 3rd was perhaps our greatest achievement. He was to sire many of our best heifers which in the course of time left their mark on our improved herd. One of his sons Mousefield Merry Monarch took the Breed Cup at Newbury Market Spring Sale and that day I proudly walked it round the ring to display the champion's rosette, listening with unbelieving ears as it was sold by auction to Clayton Ponting for one hundred guineas. Truly a stupendous sum for one of our animals at just one year old. The date April 5th 1956. Mousefield Imperial Triumph born 27.6.59 was another great young bull which was sold to Glyn Davies of South Wales. Down calving heifers surplus to our requirements were sold to farmers expanding or improving their dairy herds in different parts of the country, but whilst I later exported pigs I never sent cattle overseas.

The dairy shorthorn is a hardy, dual-purpose animal. It will breed a good beef steer, is very docile, with excellent mothering instincts and will give a fair milk yield on home produced rations in adverse weather conditions. In fact our cows laid out the year round in all weather. Some winters they entered the cowshed for the morning milking, backs covered in snow, with icicles three and four inches long hanging from their ears and shaggy, long-coated hides.

This period of my life as a breeder of pedigree livestock was interesting and rewarding. It was a sad day when the economies of the job forced me to artificially inseminate our Shorthorns with Friesian semen, in an attempt to raise milk yields. 1959-60 was the last year

81

that I registered stock in the Shorthorn Herd Book.

The black and white Friesian bull crossed with a red or roan Shorthorn cow throws a mainly black calf, for better or worse it follows that within a few years our herd changed its colour. In common with many other dairy farmers I planned to increase still further the yields from each cow and at the same time double the size of the herd. Thus we too were laying the foundation for the butter mountain of the 1980's.

Slowly I built the numbers up to forty, pushing them through the old tie-up cow stall in relays. Now it was almost a fulltime job for one person carrying milk to the dairy still using the shoulder yoke and two pails.

It was at this point in time that 'Mister Blow' joined the staff. Mister Blow certainly cut the workload greatly improving efficiency in the cow shed. Our 'new assistant' was purchased for two pounds and ten shillings. It was a simple contrivence, fitting snugly on the top of a churn of milk with a hollow metal pipe going down inside the churn almost to the bottom and back again. A rubber hose connected to a cold water supply circulated water under pressure, the internal pipe spun round thus cooling the milk whilst the next churn was being filled. At the end of the milking session I pulled full churns on a two wheeled carrier across the lawn, uphill all the way. Dora our 'dairy maid' pushing and puffing in the rear, round the farmhouse to the dairy. Here the churns were labelled with our name and address then loaded into the milk float to be taken to the farm entrance. Black Beauty, harnessed and tethered to a clothes post stamped her iron shod hooves impatient to be off. I'd clamber aboard, clasp the reins, Dora released the halter, with a snort Beauty was off to a start that would do credit to a Roman chariot race!!

In those days we received one shilling and ten pence per gallon in the spring of the year rising to perhaps two shillings and four pence in the winter. Our production varied between fifty gallons per day at turn-out time, dropping to around thirty gallons in the depth of winter.

By the early 1960's dairy farmers increasing their herds once again were building and fitting up parlours of all shapes and sizes (Government Grants freely available) although quite a few were still milking cows through a Hosier Bale out on the Downs or by standing a bale on a concrete standing in the shelter of their farm buildings.

I did neither, I still favoured making use of our existing stoutly built brick and tile cowshed. By now I had a wife and six children to support, there was no way I could go round the agricultural shows looking with envy at fabulously expensive milking parlours, yet I realised that in some way I had to move with the times. Bulk tanks with direct pipeline milking were coming in fast, churns were on their way out, no mistake about that.

I purchased through the 'House of Toomer' a secondhand 'Fullwood Parlour Adaptor'. Using our own labour we dismantled this contraption of rubbers, pipes and metal sheets from a local farm. Transported home in the cattle truck it was assembled into the far end of the cowshed.

It accommodated six cows, held in place by a chain round their hindquarters. Three feed hoppers held about five hundred-weight each of concentrates which was dispensed with a measured hand scoop. Now with the bucket redundant, milk was conveyed through an overhead stainless steel pipe to the 150 gallon bulk tank.

In farming circles we had gone bulk. Receiving an extra predecimalization penny per gallon on our monthly milk cheque. The 'tanker' came each day, the driver coupled up a long flexible pipe draining out our daily production in a few minutes. What progress from the days of Beauty and the milk float!!

Our simple parlour-adaptor served the purpose for ten or twelve years but our dairy herd, now all black and white, had expanded to sixty in number,

The next step up the ladder of progress was a Hosier 10-10. This was erected in the corner of the yard with work commencing on April 3rd, 1973. A new collecting yard was constructed and we worked under great difficulty with the cows still using the old system. An open field site on new ground would have been much easier and perhaps more sensible but once again shortage of capital was the governing factor,

Tim, Richard, Jane and the rest of the family set to preparing the site. It was pick and shovel work, breaking up the existing concrete yard.

Dartmoor convicts couldn't have toiled harder. All through April work progressed until on May 14th Tim moved the new parlour into place.

Dora as usual gave vent to her opinion, casting grave doubts about, "milking down in a pit". "We shall all get plastered with cow dung and kicked in the head, you see, and I don't think I shall be able to reach their teats" she continued. I tried to reassure her, "Yes you will Dora, we will stand you on a concrete block if necessary".

June 29th, 1973 was the big day. My son Tim, my wife and I attempted the milking. What a shindy it was too, those stubborn cows just would not enter our bright spotless new parlour. When they did after much pushing, shoving and swearing on our part, they just refused to let down any milk despite the fact that we constantly tempted them with concentrates from the overhead feed store!

For Dora it was her third milking system at Mousefield Farm. I always maintained it took us longer to train Dora than it did the cows, but once mastered she was forced to agree there were advantages over the old method.

The Hosier parlour proved to be cold and draughty in winter, hot and stuffy in summer and flies were a menace in July and August. However milking was completed much quicker and with the advantage of automatic circulation cleaning, I could quietly abscond to my breakfast rasher and egg, letting the chore of washing through the pipeline and clusters take care of itself!

I gave up milking cows myself after the sudden death of my dear wife on January 17th 1976. Prior to that date I had missed few milkings in forty-six years except for the war period.

My second son Tony milked fulltime for a while, living at that time in 'Redlands' our farm bungalow. Then there was a period from July 1979 to July 1980 when Stephen my youngest son was in complete charge of our dairy herd, a most responsible task and, although he had his ups and downs, he succeeded in pushing the cows to a new peak of production.

Tim was next to take up the challenge with plans to expand the herd to two hundred head, milking through a completely new Fullwood 20/20, fully automated herringbone parlour with computerised feeding. The automation included cluster removers, flow meters and vacuum operated gates.

Demolition of the old cart shed to make room for the new set-up started in spring 1982.

Doing most of the construction work with our own labour it was the largest and most expensive project we had ever undertaken, costing in the region of £50,000.

Cowman's Code

The cow is queen, so don't forget,
Don't curse or swear, or make her fret.
Talk quietly, and treat her well;
Your profits then are sure to swell.

Don't raise your voice, don't move too quick.
Don't make her run. Don't use that stick.
Then with quiet confidence instilled
You'll see your bulk tank better filled.

And if, perchance, Kate kicks your arm,
Don't kick her back, she meant no harm.
Just pat her gently, calm her fear,
And softly say "I love you dear."

And when she dungs all o'er the floor,
Just wash it down and through the door.
Don't stamp your feet and throw abuse.
Perhaps she's ill - a trifle loose ?

And as you walk among your herd
Remember, stop-have a word
With Jessie, Flo, and Snowy too.
It's not so much to ask of you.

Always bear these words in mind;
As you improve, you're sure to find,
Your cows will lie content, and so
Abundantly the milk will flow.

Composed during milking by Mr Anthony Houghton, dairy farmer, of Long Lane, Newbury, Berks, after reading "When familiarity breeds content", in Farmers Weekly, July, 1975.

Hard at work on the new parlour

Members of my family worked like slaves for many months. Tim laying upwards of seven thousand concrete blocks. My youngest daughter Bobby worked as bricklayer's mate during school holidays. Richard laid concrete almost by the acre, after completing drains and the parlour working pit. Eventually the latest, most modern milking set-up at Mousefield Farm was ready to be christened.

Bringing out a bottle of the best, a toast was drunk to what, at present, we like to think is the last word in dairy technology. Dora was still with us after thirty-seven years as 'cow girl', not tipping milk anymore, but still able to tip a glass of scotch!! November 1982 we switched to milking three times a day, every eight hours the electric motor started up, it seemed that production never stopped, indeed there was precious little time during the twenty-four hour day that our hard pressed bovine charges were not entering or leaving the parlour. One could almost imagine one cow saying to her neighbour, "Oh, blast it my dear its milking time again, one hardly gets time to enjoy a bite of grass these days, and I've not had a decent night's sleep for months. They have even sent the bull for slaughter, all we are going to get is a gent in a plastic mac from the artificial insemination centre once a year. There's just no fun left in our lives anymore, not like the old days when we could do a bit of courting under the oak trees".

This caper came to an end for us with the introduction of milk quotas in April 1984.

Quotas were fixed at 1983 production less 9% but, because of our previous high level of production, our allocation was over one million litres per year.

I wonder, where does the milk industry go from here? What innovation will we witness in the last decade of the twentieth century?

Meeting the dairy cows milk potential, maintaining herd fertility and overall health are fundamental to a successful dairy business. Profitable milk production depends on correct feeding in early lactation to enable the cow to reach peak yields and get back in calf at the right time. Even now the boffins are talking and writing of a gene-splicing breakthrough that could shortly revolutionise the economies of dairy farming. The first commercial sales could soon take place of bovine somatotropin (BST), a genetic growth hormone that offers increases in milk yields of 15-20% without extra feed costs. Farmers will be able to produce more milk from fewer cows, but where will that road lead us?

With the possible exception of a few isolated areas every household in the British Isles can get their daily requirement of milk delivered to their doorstep almost every day of the year. This unique service demands great toil from the dairy farmer and his devoted staff, not forgetting the tanker drivers, processors and of course the local roundsmen, who often set off on their rounds by 4 am.

'Milk, the complete food' must surely be the housewife's best buy of the week?

Dora, and myself have, thankfully, retired from the rat race leaving the problems to the next generation.

My well worn milking stool now resides in the TV room used only to support a cup of coffee and my cheese and biscuits at supper time!!

Growing and harvesting roots

Thirty odd years ago, which takes me back to pre-1960, our expanding dairy herd, with followers of all ages got through literally mountains of food during the long winter months.

The policy was to be self-supporting in feeding stuffs for our stock, after all it was not many years previous that purchased animal feed was available only on coupons! Strictly rationed in other words, a fact difficult to comprehend in this day and age of massive grain mountains. In addition to well made hay, roots were the mainstay for the winter feed, but growing a root crop involved a considerable amount of back-breaking hand work.

We were 'green' in those days in the environmental sense, relying on an abundance of farmyard manure to maintain soil fertility and science had not come up with sprays to control weeds in kale, mangels, fodder beet or swedes without killing the crop itself.

Today we have switched from labour intensive roots to maize silage for winter stock feed, drilling and harvesting almost a hundred acres, yet maize is not a new crop to Mousefield, I grew it in the fifties. Two or three acres, some years it grew eight feet tall which we cut green with a sickle and carted to the cows in the dry spell of August-September when the grass gave up on our sandy soil.

Marrow stem kale followed on, then thousand-head which withstood the frost better. Either could and did taint the milk if fed in excess. Swedes are good cow grub but being a hard root required being put through the pulper. These sliced roots were mixed with rolled barley, a time-consuming business. During the hungry months of March and April our large outdoor clamps of mangels came into their own. Mangels bigger'n footballs were fed whole to the milkers. Ours cows just loved to munch their way through juicy mangelwurzels. Opponents of the crop claimed it was an expensive way to water cows! "Mangolds be ninety per cent water" was their argument. However it must be rather special water because our cows held their milk yields well on mangels and hay until May turn-out.

Roots demand plenty of well rotted farmyard manure. The previous winter's muck, stored through the summer in conveniently placed stacks was loaded onto a tractor trailer or horse drawn wagon by the laborious use of four grained long-handled forks. Transported to autumn corn stubble small piles of dung were spaced out, pulled off the trailer by the use of a drag fork. Slowly the whole field was covered in neat straight lines, each heap five strides from the next. When this 'natural plant food' was spread on the ground by hand-fork it gave a complete even covering which was then ploughed in before autumn rains made the land too wet. Winter rain, frost and snow contributed to a fine tilth in spring.

The successful growing of a root crop requires well drained fertile soil, seeds drilled in a well prepared seed bed at the appropriate time, keeping on top of the weed and pest problem and the type of English weather that doesn't go down well with families on summer holidays!!

In my early farming days, I pushed a single row root drill. The wheels set out so that on the return bout, by following the previous wheelmark one got an even spacing between each row of seeds. From that primitive method I progressed to a four row horse drill – later to be converted to tractor drawn.

Thursday was, and still is market day in Newbury. Farmers didn't spend all their day in the livestock section or the nearby pub, equally important to them was the Corn Exchange standing in its prominent position in the market square. My father always made it his business to visit the Corn Exchange on market day even if he had no grain to buy or sell. As a teenager I accompanied him on these visits, feeling most important as we passed through the big front door of the imposing facade. Through an inner doorway one stepped into a vast open area with a very high roof, around three sides, some two or three yards apart stood corn and seed merchants business stands each with the name of the trading firm proudly displayed. New Bros Ltd; H Dolton & Son; Chas Midwinter & Sons; Toogoods; Berks, Bucks and Oxen Farmers Ltd; Smith Chamberhouse Mill, Thatcham; and a score of others long since passed into obscurity. Behind each, dressed in well tailored suits stood the firms representative, keen as mustard to conduct business. Farmers brought in their grain samples in tiny bags, minute examination of individual grains for plumpness, colour, smooth skin, followed by a moisture test, told the prospective buyer whether he was handling an excellent, middling or indifferent grain sample,

My father liked to visit the Corn Exchange mainly to keep a tag on feeding stuff prices. We never had any large parcels of grain to sell so we didn't count for much. The 'Big Boys' with their malting samples got most attention.

I have mentioned the Corn Exchange because of its importance in those days to the general trade of the area, when Newbury was truly a rural market town. The building still stands, silently awaiting its fate whilst planners argue over its future role. (1990)

The traders, middle-aged men, when I was in my youth, will by now have all passed on leaving few who can remember the scene as thousands of tons of grain, fertilizer and livestock feed changed hands.

Back in those days February or early March was the time we purchased our root seed. Entering the Exchange it soon became apparent that at this time of the year father and I got more attention. Competition was strong and it was a wellknown fact that dad's money was good!

Kale seed cost three shillings and sixpence per lb. Drilled at the rate of four pounds to the acre gave a total cost of fourteen shillings (70 pence since decimalisation) to plant an acre (4840 square yards). Mangel seed cost slightly more.

My father would try two or three merchants for price, after which we usually purchased from 'Toogoods' who had a reputation for top quality, although more expensive. Not surprising this often saved money at the end of the day, due to good germination one could get a good plant from less seed.

Seeds planted late April early May quickly showed drill, unfortunately the weeds were quick to follow!!

Most seasons the first two delicate green leaves of the tiny kale plant were attacked by the flea beetle resulting in the whole field of new plants being completely destroyed if counter measures were not taken promptly. In those days there were no sprays or powder to deal with this minute pest, which multiplied in vast numbers, especially if thundery conditions prevailed.

Most farmers who grew brassica crops had their own pet solution to the problem. Some continually rolled the crop with a Cambridge Roller, others dragged sacks soaked in paraffin over the ground. I adopted my father's method. 'Catch the little buggers on a tar pole!'

A long wooden pole some 20 feet long had a small wheel fastened at each end. The whole length of this pole had 'West of England' corn sacks nailed to it which dragged behind. On the pole and undersides of the sacks we smeared tar. Thick, black, sticky stuff. With my sister Delcie's help, we pulled this weird contraption up and down the field keeping the pole some six inches above the threatened plants. As pole and sacks passed over the ground the flea beetles jumped up onto the tar pole in their thousands from which there was no escape. Twice, or three times a day we covered the ground until the threat to our crop had receded. We didn't always win, on occasions the sheer number of beetles won the battle which meant replanting, an expensive business.

Weeds, weeds and yet more weeds, untold hours of arduous toil was needed just to keep abreast of the problem. It is true that there were selective weedkiller on the market, but in those days they couldn't be used safely on root crops.

Couch, fat hen, charlock, buttercup, kemp nettle, poppy, chickweed, thistles, docks, bindweed, all attempted to crowd out our young crop if given the slightest chance to get the upper hand.

The first task was to flat hoe between the rows until the young plants were large enough to 'cut' out. With kale it wasn't necessary to be too precise to single out each plant but with mangels, fodder beet or swedes a single plant every twelve to fifteen inches was the norm.

It requires considerable dexterity of wrists and eye to flash an eight inch blade between a row of small delicate plants leaving just one standing in the correct place. It was back-aching work under a hot sun.

If the weeds looked like getting the upper hand, I called in Amos Black. With his wife, children and other members of this local gypsy family they made up a sizeable team.

Amos lived in a converted bus, his parents in a beautifully decorated horse drawn caravan, resplendent in its highly polished brass and brilliantly painted woodwork.

These travelling casual workers toured the district coming back year after year to the same farms. They flat-hoed for two pounds ten shilling per acre, cut out for three pounds Their day started soon after dawn, when the air was sweet and cool, working almost non-stop until noon, bent low over their flashing short-handled hoes one behind the other, each moving swiftly down a row, not straightening their backs until reaching the headland at the far end.

Lunch break beneath the shade of a large oak tree often lasted two hours or more. Time to get a fire going. A large black pot hung from an iron tripod over the flames. Into the simmering brown coloured liquid went taties, dumplings, vegetables and other myste-rious ingredients. "Only I knows the secret of what goes into that pot governor," stressed Mrs Black, looking at me with her dark brown eyes beneath jet black hair. The skin of their faces taunt and tanned a leathery brown from a life-time spent in the open air.

Many a time my wife Peggy and I joined them at the midday break and were invited to sample the contents of the pot, at the same time enjoy a joke and savour stories of their way of life, as they trav-elled the countryside always on the move.

Their ability to live off the land was astonishing, possessing knowledge of which wild fruits, berries and nuts made good eating, which mushrooms and fungi were non-poisonous. These travelling vagabonds always had a mongrel dog or two trained to sniff out a rabbit or even a hedgehog slumbering under leaves. The latter, despatched with a sharp blow on the head, these small creatures were next rolled in clay and cooked in the red embers of the fire. On removing the baked clay the protective stiff spines peeled off to reveal sulculent juicy meat.

So much for our casual workers, they did a good job, expected ready cash, paid no taxes, would argue over acreage and ask for extra if it had taken them longer than anticipated, but all in all we looked forward to their annual visit,

After the root crop had been flat-hoed and singled out the young plants were away to a good start but it was still essential to keep abreast of the weeds.

One of my pictures on the farmhouse wall shows Roy Adnams aged sixteen leading Beauty our light farm horse pulling a single row horse hoe with myself keeping the heavy iron frame on course between the rows of plants,

I used this method until 1955, when our last working horse was

The author with the last working horse Black Beauty

sold. Beauty newly shod, groomed and looking immaculate was driven to Reading horse auction, which to this day still takes place on the first Friday in the month.

It was a sad day and tears were shed, but such is the price of 'progress' down on the farm. Beauty made forty guineas. The rubber tyred milk float five shillings and the set of beautifully polished harness which Dora had spent the best part of the previous day cleaning raised the magnificent sum of two shillings. Ten pence in today's money, and we had the auctioneers commission to pay out of that!!

In 1955 I purchased a brand new Ferguson T 20 for £575. My parents considered I was completely mad, the wayward son spending his father's hard earned cash with abandonment. This lovable little tractor soon proved itself, doing ten times the work in a day that our one horse power unit had previously managed. With three-point linkage and hydraulic lift I had really gone to town in farm mechanisation! The next purchase was a four-row Ferguson steerage hoe.

Model B-KE 20 with disc costing £86. Developed to perform a high standard of close cultivation, through a wide range of row widths. The tractor driver needed to look well ahead and steer as centrally between the rows as possible. The second operator sat on a low sprung seat and by means of the steering arm bracket guided the hoe blades either side of the rows of plants.

As the growing season progressed the leaves of our crops now covered the ground. Our battle against weeds finally won.

Come October it was harvest time for mangels. Eighty per cent of a mangel grows above ground which makes for easy lifting. With one's right hand moving clockwise you grasp the leafy crown. A curved serrated-edged knife in the left hand sliced off the leaves and in one quick movement the mangel was deftly placed in a central heap. Each pile was then covered with the cut leaves to give some protection against early autumn frosts. The roots were left in these small heaps for two or three weeks to mature until carted and stacked. The best bet was to store them in the big barn with straw bales for protection, here they were conveniently placed for winter feeding. We couldn't store all our crop under cover which meant constructing an outdoor clamp. First a trench was dug by pick and shovel, two feet wide, a foot deep marking out the intended site. This was to act as a drain to run off rainwater and at the same time provide some soil to seal our mangel clamp against frost, but first an insulating layer of wheat straw was laid thatch like on the roots.

In the early days of my farming career, I used our two shire horses and a heavy scotch-cart, with tipping gear, to move the crop from field to store, later by tractor and trailer. Every mangel loaded by hand, either way it certainly involved a great deal of heavy back-aching labour.

Copper or Gold

For fifty years I bred, fattened and traded in pigs. To say that I kept pigs would be incorrect, more truthfully they not only kept me but my large family as well.

There has always been that recurring succession between prosperity and depression in the pig market. Copper or gold, muck or money. When pigs were expensive and showing profit farmers and pig keepers rushed to buy, thus forcing up the price of store pigs even further or else they expanded their pig breeding unit. The pig is a most prolific animal which means that in a short period of time a healthy profit turns to crippling losses caused by the inevitable glut of finished pigs awaiting slaughter.

My aim was that my pigs returned muck and money. The only way to achieve that objective in my opinion is to stay with pigs through thick and thin, weather the storm and sure enough the sun will shine once more but sometimes it can be an awful long wait!

Pigs; hundreds, thousands of them. Fat ones, thin ones, black, white, blue, ginger and every cross in between passed through our Danish piggery over the years. The lucky ones enjoyed our hospitality for a few months, some a few weeks but the vast majority just overnight for bed, breakfast and a bath. People tend to think of the pig as a dirty animal, when actually they are perhaps the cleanest of our domesticated farm stock. In the old days when most farmers and allotment holders reared a few pigs many failed to understand this simple fact, and kept their pigs in filth with little or no litter and in draughty, leaky buildings, often forced to sell because they were losing money. Nevertheless my father and I had the reputation for paying fair prices. The deal was struck, money changed hands, then our newly acquired stock had to be loaded for transport. Not always an easy task, the number of times a small pig keeper built his makeshift piggery at the far end of an allotment or at the lowest point of a sloping, wet, boggy field, far from the hard road with no thought whatever as to how he intended to get his stock to market. "How we going to load these twenty weaners then Arthur?" I'd ask. Having received good money on a poor market for his pigs it was a matter of absolute priority to get them onto the waiting wagon. "Now don't worry, my pigs are very quiet. If I gets a bucket with a few nuts to rattle they'll follow me anywhere," says our farmer friend. I have my doubts, across the field maybe, but experience tells me they will not venture up the steep slope of the lorry tailboard. Not wise to argue, the owner knows best. Full of confidence Arthur opens the sty gate, out swarms our latest purchase, only to scatter in every direction, barking with pleasure at their release from prison as only pigs can. "Tig, tig, tig" calls the optimistic pig-keeper as he marches ahead frantically rattling the bucket handle. My father and I struggle along in the rear, each of us carrying a ten foot long sheet of galvanised tin as we try desperately to contain those future pork sausages still jumping, mock-fighting and barking with glee. After much running, cursing and sweating profusely, somehow more by luck than anything else we succeed in getting them onto the lorry tailboard. "There you are, told you we could do it" says Arthur with some exhileration. "Go steady, don't be too sure, they're not in yet" I say. When loading pigs, "there is always one" we used to say. Sure enough this time is no exception. At the last moment one makes a break for freedom, squeezing through a gap in our sheets of tin, "Damn and blast, you've let one go" says Arthur. With that they all turn and make a mad dash for home knocking my father flying into the mud. Getting to his feet, he's quick to weigh up the situation. "There's only one thing for it, we shall have to carry them pigs one at a time to get 'im loaded. "What a bloody stupid place to build a pigsty." This from my father who was not given to swearing.

Safely loaded at last we are on the way home. "Never worth it, buying pigs from that man, let somebody else have the trouble next time" says dad. Yet I know for sure, in six months time when the next two litters are ready for sale we would be there again whatever the trade or the weather.

Back at home I reverse carefully to the unloading bay of the piggery. My mother comes out to the garden gate and shouts, "You two coming in, its getting late and the supper is spoiling." Better go I 'spose" says dad sheepishly. "We'll come out later to see these new pigs."

Later we return once more to the piggery. This time carrying a small churn of warm soapy water which is poured into an old fashioned tin bath. With ear-piercing squeals each piglet is washed and scrubbed to be followed by a good square meal, then a deep bed of best wheat straw in the luxury of our fully insulated building completes the process. Next morning their previous owner would fail to recognise his own stock.

Taken on the forty-five mile journey to Guildford livestock market in our cattle truck those well presented, well travelled weaners make pounds more than we had paid for them. Homeward bound we pull into a quiet layby to partake of a late lunch. "Trade was good today dad." We both agreed it had been a profitable transaction.

Our county town of Reading held its livestock market every Saturday and Monday throughout the year. It often happened that my father and I were asked to purchase stock after the auction closed. One occasion comes to mind. A certain George Tyler had two fat hogs for sale. We were to follow him as he led the way. He drove ahead in a much battered car twisting and turning through the back streets in the direction of Caversham until, leaving the rows of terraced houses behind we emerged at some allotments near the River Thames. As was often the case the sty was built at least a hundred yards from the nearest hard road. It is so easy for someone to purchase two young piglets and carry them in their arms with no thought of the day that they will have to leave.

Those two pigs were now enormous, they could hardly turn round in their tiny home, obviously all they did in life was eat and sleep, they should have gone to a bacon factory months ago. It was plain to see that their owner didn't have the faintest idea how he could get them there. Two pairs of pink eyes, almost hidden in layers of fat looked up at us. They immediately recognised George and started squealing in unison expecting yet more food.

"Told you I had two grand pigs over here didn't I, so t'wasn't a wasted journey, now how much you going to give me for them?" says our friend. "You have kept them too long and overfed them George." Butchers don't like fat these days, the public will not buy

Gentle persuasion

rashers with two inches of fat on them. Twenty pounds each, thats if we can get them into our lorry" I replied. "No, them's worth more'n that, give me £50 and there'er yours". "Can't be done George, we got to get them down to Harris of Calne, only place I know take such heavy pigs, couldn't be giving you £40 only we have a load to take on Monday." "Ok there'er yours, lets load 'em up."

"It is not going to be as simple as that." I replied. "Pity we can't get the lorry to the sty, only way is to walk them one at a time, tie a rope to their hind leg then if they decide to make a break for it we got a line on them." This plan succeeds, we get the first pig to the tailramp, but would it go up that slope, not on your life. It dug its feet into the ground, just refusing to budge. The more we pushed on its backside the more it squealed in protest. George cursed and swore calling his pet pig all the names under the sun. He knew that if he couldn't get his two plump pigs into our lorry he wasn't going to get his forty quid. "I'm beat you" says George. "They be never going to walk up, and 'tiss plain we can't carry 'em,"

My father was not a man to be beaten by a stubborn pig. "Got a dustbin George?" he asks. "No 'fraid not, but I can get a swill bin if that'll do". Whilst he rushed to get the required item our pig, no doubt thinking the battle won had wandered off and was busy rooting up an absent allotment holder's early potatoes!

Back again with the greasy, unwashed swill bin he hands it to my father. "Here you are, but I can't think what you are going to do with it, or how its going to help load these pigs." Dad takes the bin. "Now you two, do as I tell you, George get hold of that pig's tail and turn its arse to the tailboard." With that dad pushes the swill bin over the pig's snout. "Quick, grab t'other handle Bert". With George steering the rear end the pig, now in reverse tried to extract itself from the unexpected blindfold walked backwards up the loading ramp. George shook his head in disbelief. "Well I be damned, I'd never had thought it possible, who taught you that trick Frank?"

"Let's go and get t'other 'un or we will be here 'til dark."

Come Monday morning those two now docile, fat hogs are reloaded once more, no trouble this time going up the ramp with twenty or thirty others. An hour later they are bedded down in clean wood shavings in the lairage at 'Harris of Calne' quietly awaiting their fate. "Oh, how sad, how could you do it?" I've often heard this said. In reply I say, "Well, you all like sausages, pork pies and best back bacon don't you?"

Sheep Farming

Royal Berkshire is surely one of the most beautiful counties of England. Old Father Thames meanders through lush, green meadows grazed by contented cattle, whilst wooded hills rise steeply on either side at the point where the river breached the chalk wall of the Corallian Ridge some seventy million years ago, to form Goring Gap. Further down stream the Royal residence of Windsor Castle dominates the south bank. Rich farm lands abound in the Thames, Kennet and Lambourn valleys, fertile soil that grows bounteous crops year after year, whilst to the north of the county stretches the vast, desolate expanse of the rolling Berkshire Downs. Frequently uncomfortable in summer, bleak in winter yet still it is an enchanted land, with tranquil, olde worlde villages hidden away, aloof from the mad rush of modern traffic. It is the county with the shape of an old boot, at least it was until neighbouring Oxfordshire pinched the northern section cutting it off at the ankle and with the same stroke rustling our one and only prehistoric White Horse of Uffington, gouged from the turf of the Downs by ancient man.

Berkshire was, and still is, a great county for sheep. In the thirteenth and fouteenth centuries the wool brought prosperity to the area and many of the fine old churches were built by successful wool merchants. In its Tudor heyday perhaps the best known was 'Jack of Newbury' whose wealth, 'from the backs of little sheep' rebuilt St Nicholas Church, during and after his lifetime.

I lay no claim to being much of a shepherd, having always preferred working with our milk cows and their offspring. Even the pigs won second place in the livestock stakes on our farm. Be that as it may, I must be one of the very few farmers left in the area with a vivid memory of the great East Ilsley Sheep Fairs. The last auction was held in 1934. In the early nineteen thirties, as a twelve year old

Sheep sale at Ilsley

I frequently accompanied my father to these fortnightly sales. (School was never that important to me.) It was a wonderful sight, the usually sleepy little village teemed with life and noise. Thousands of sheep arrived there on foot and were packed tightly into little pens on either side of the street and in the fields around, sheltered from the elements under trees planted for that very purpose. The sheep dogs drove their charges into the pens, shepherds cursed and shouted and the frightened sheep baa-ed their heads off.

Selling started very early in the morning, my father and I left home at the crack of dawn in the horse drawn trap, pulled by his favourite horse, a little black cob called Dick, who made short work of the twelve mile journey. Dad didn't usually bring many sheep home, in the main he bought for other farmers, who had neither the time nor the inclination to attend this bustling event.

My father taught me much that has added pleasure, interest and enlightenment to my life. From him I learnt much of the age-old wisdom of the countryside, yet he was true and just in all his dealings, an excellent example to any young man making his way in the world. His advice and kind recommendations proved invaluable to me in later life. During the morning dad always met up with his business associate, Harry Larkcom, and this frequently ended up in a visit to one of the many public houses. If my memory serves me correctly this was either at the Crown and Horn or the Swan on the opposite side of the street. Because of my age I was not allowed inside the pub but sat outside on a wooden bench with a glass of lemonade and a small loaf of bread and cheese, as often as not it was not long before I fell asleep, oblivious to the crowd of drovers, dealers, farmers and sheep who thronged the narrow village street.

One could hire a drover with a dog for a small sum and, even before the auction was over, many of the sheep were started off to their new home driven down some of the numerous narrow, green banked roads that linked each district. It was my job to walk in front, the shepherd and his dog drove the sheep and dad brought up the rear surveying all from the high seat in the trap. I suppose he made a few pounds from his sheep deals, he always seemed in a good mood and talked of little else for the next few days!

Every farm of any size owned a breeding flock and one of the first jobs in the New Year was to make the lambing pen. Built in the form of a square and constructed with wooden hurdles, lined and thatched with straw they were beautiful to look at, very warm and cosy. Little square pens just big enough for a ewe and her lamb. If a lamb died or was born dead it was skinned and the skin immediately tied onto another lamb, taken from a 'double' or 'triplet'. The mother would sniff it hard for a while, then the little creature would start suckling and wagging its tail vigorously. They would settle down peacefully together, and all would be well.

Our sheep flock in those days comprised of little more than fifty or so broken mouth ewes and their lambs but even that small number made much work. We were always worming, drenching, dagging, shearing them, or some other foolishness, and on far too many occasions digging a hole to bury one that had just given up the will to live. Sheep have a nasty habit of dying for no apparent reason and if they don't succumb to one of the many diseases that can afflict them it is not unknown to find one drowned in the water trough. Another favourite form of suicide is to roll over onto their backs in some small hollow in the ground, unable to right themselves, especially if heavy in-lamb, they soon die if the shepherd isn't vigilant. The stray dog is a deadly menace. When the owner is brought to book they often say "oh, but my dog is very quiet, just a soppy pet, he certainly wouldn't injure a sheep". The fact is a dog or dogs often act in play with the sheep and don't always cause physical injury but as the flock stampede to a corner of the field or through the fence in terror stress will cause pregnant ewes to abort thus destroying a whole year's work of the farmer.

The late Micky Werrall of Hampstead Norreys came to our farm each year to shear our ewes and the two rams. It was this worthy country gentleman who taught me the art of sheep shearing. It was also possible to learn a much wider vocabulary of swear words especially if the shearing didn't go well!

I suppose I must have been fourteen years old when I was given my first lesson in how to remove a fleece from a sheep using the old fashioned hand clippers. It is no easy task to caste a big ewe, hold her steady between one's knees and at the same time remove a year's growth of wool.

It was the second week in May, the ewes and their lambs had been rounded up the previous evening, held overnight under cover in case of rain. The sheep had to be dry for shearing. The lambs would not be shorn of course,but stayed with their mothers until each ewe was pulled out for clipping, then they kicked up a hell of a shindy.

Mr Werrall came up the farm drive at 7.30 am. We knew he wouldn't be late, he worked long days at this time of the year. Preparations were soon made, Micky tied a leather apron round his waist, then produced two pairs of clippers from an old sack. Turning to me he said, "yer yah be, me bwoy, gwona larn you the tricks ole the trade this season, time you could shear a yowl or two, what be fouteen this time bissent. Catch a small un to start wee." With that I grasped a ewe, sat it on its backside holding it firmly between my knees. Micky had also caught a ewe. "Now lad, watch me and do the same as I. Start clipping like this, first along its belly round the shoulder and up round the neck, then repeat that line again. Keep the yowl's head held tight over yer knee with tother 'and, then she can't move. You got to get the fleece off in one piece remember." Snip, snip, snip its not so easy as it looks by any means. I was terribly slow and every now and again, I'm afraid, I snicked the ewe's skin drawing blood which made her wince. I had got about half the fleece removed and was clipping round her neck when 'it' happened. I clipped the top of the poor creatures ear off. That did it. She just exploded into the air, a struggling mass of mutton, legs and wool. I lost my grip, she landed upright and promptly took off across the meadow like a rocket. She sort of bounced along, all four feet well clear of the ground at times, she was in a hell of a temper and trailing behind her was half a fleece, someones future woollen sweater. I stood in a state of shock, mouth agape, well aware of what to expect from my tutor. "Drat me boots, you've gone and let the darn thing go." "I'm sorry Micky, I snicked its ear and it just took off like." "Course the poor sod did, so would you if I cut your y'ear off. Well, don't just stand there bwoy, get a-gwain, round the bloody thing up and back into the 'olding pen. Bless me, weres me dawg? Tess, Tess away there."

I finally sheared that ewe and four or five more before the sun went down, but by golly it had been a hectic day. I couldn't stand up straight, my arms and fingers ached like nobody's business. I was hungry, thirsty, dirty, greasy and wet with sweat but I also experienced an inner satisfaction, a day of achievement. Wiping my brow I muttered, "I don't know about you Micky but I'm whacked." "Don't make such a fuss me bwoy, you'll live, hard work never killed nobody" was all he said. This short chapter on sheep spans a period of over half a century. I'm the old man now.

With the passing years our farm witnessed the steady expansion in the dairy herd with the result that our interest in the sheep waned and for a long spell the woollies were given a miss. Not until Spring '87, when my two sons were firmly in charge of the farming operations, did we once again take up the role of shepherd. It all came about with the offer of grazing on the new site of the Newbury and Royal County of Berkshire Show ground. Reseeded, fertilized and well rolled it was marvellous grazing land. "Richard and I are thinking of going into sheep in a big way dad" announced my son Tim one Spring morning. He continued to outline their plan with enthusiasm. This was to purchase three hundred mule two-tooths with lambs at foot – couples as they are called, even if a ewe has twins or even triplets. Then next back end the lambs would be sold off fat so we would bring the ewes back to the farm to winter on stubble turnips and our downland pasture. Come November we could put them to Charolais rams to produce top quality lambs the following Spring. This would provide a useful income over and above the monthly milk cheque.

They asked me what I thought and with no desire to stamp on the ambition of youth, I replied. "Have a go by all means if you wish, you'll learn the hard way thats for sure, sheep farming is no push-over." With that we were back into sheep, but this time in a much more professional way. The sale of sixty prime bullocks brought in a tidy sum. Thirty thousand pounds in fact and my sons blew the lot on a flock of sheep and equipment! The Bank Manager raised the roof, he'd been reckoning on the money from the sale of our beef to clear our overdraft. At the end of the day as Managing Director I would be held responsible to the bank if our family firm went bust!

To give credit where credit is due, my two lads did succeed, yet not without a great deal of hard work and many anxious moments, I may add. Night after night at lambing time one or the other worked 'til dawn, delivering lambs under a brilliant arc lamp, with all the usual problems. Difficult births, prolapses, ewes that refused to accept their own offspring, others that completely ignored the first born when the second arrived, ewes with a large stillborn lamb and others with too many.

We had our ups and downs like everyone else but by and large this latest venture into sheep has been successful and modestly prof-itable. Unfortunately the severe summer drought of 1990 proved a disaster for our sheep flock. Grass gave up growing completely, we made no hay and little silage. The ewes had no milk, the lambs stood still. In the end we sent five hundred ewes and lambs to graze my step-son's lush green pastures in Lancashire. In my opinion sheep farming for us is on the way out once more!

Before closing this chapter on sheep I must mention wool. When my wife Ruth and I toured New Zealand, at almost every farm we visited the lady of the house was an expert with the spinning wheel and it wasn't long before Ruth was taking lessons in the art of spin-ning wool.

We brought two of those beautiful Merino fleeces home with us, crammed so tightly into one of our cases that the only way we could shut the lid was by sucking out the air with a vacuum cleaner! If Customs & Excise had made us open it, goodness knows how we would have closed it again.

We now had the wool but without a spinning wheel no further progress could be made. "I will make enquiries, and at the same time look out for one" I said hopefully. With that the matter was forgotten in the busy round of farm life.

The last leaves of autumn were clinging to the oaks. The sharp frost of recent nights had weakened their hold and the next strong breeze would blow them into untidy piles around the houses. A hazy sun, low in the sky, cast long shadows as I returned in my cattle lorry from a visit to Gloucester livestock market. Passing slowly through the main street of that delightful little town of Moreton-in-Marsh, I chanced to glance in the window of an antique shop and the centrepiece was a beautiful spinning wheel, but it was getting late in the day and the shop was closed.

On arriving home I related the day's events and prices at the market, but kept quiet about my discovery in the shop window. The next day I told Ruth that I intended taking her, my mother and my mother-in-law, who was staying with us for a while, on a mystery tour of the Cotswolds. I think the ladies were beginning to doubt my sanity. Why should I suddenly take it into my head to drive aimlessly across the country in a Landrover when there were far more important tasks on the farm. Not until I pulled up outside the shop was the reason for this jaunt realised. Abruptly, it occurred to me that it was perhaps, after all, a foolhardy venture, I didn't even know the price or if it was still in working condition. To my enquiries the good lady in the shop said, "The price was £250. No she couldn't guarantee that it would work and still spin wool." Ruth with her money-conscious Lancashire upbringing was wary of spending so much money on a mere spinning wheel even if it did look like a nice piece of craftsmanship. Disregarding her advice I parted with my hard-earned cash. We returned to Mousefield in triumph, the precious spinning wheel in the rear, the ladies chatting away with visions of skeins of home-spun wool waiting to be knitted into socks, scarves and innumerous multi-pattern pullovers,

There were a few minor repairs required. A spool was missing, I got a friend, handy with a lathe to turn out another. Ruth was now all set to go, but although the wheel worked it spun the wool unevenly and in an erratic fashion. Other visiting spinning ladies tried their hand with Ruth's wheel but couldn't solve the problem. Had I bought a 'pig-in-a poke'?

It was not until we took a day off to visit the 'Bath & West Show' the following spring that quite by chance the riddle was solved. A group of spinners were demonstrating their skill. Amongst the line up of six was just one gentleman and he had a wheel identical to ours – and it worked to perfection! In answer to Ruth's query on her wheel's imperfection, one of the questions he asked was "Did she use two separate cords to drive the big wheel from the foot pedal?" "Yes", Ruth replied. "Well that could be the reason it spins as it does. You must only have one long cord and be sure it crosses over itself at the top of the run" was his suggestion.

To our surprise the problem of unevenly spun wool was solved at last.

In the long dark winter evenings as the wailing wind, driving rain and ferocious snow blizzards renew their onslaught with unabating fury, Ruth sits busy at her Rolls-Royce in spinning wheels. My vision of beautiful home-spun and hand knitted garments has come true, as for myself I keep busy writing yet more true, countryside stories.

Summer 1984, Mousefield. Ruth spins with a fleece from New Zealand.

The Farm Sale

This chapter reflects my memories of many such sales attended over the years.

The farm sale is more than just a means for the disposal of a farmer's live and deadstock. Whilst it is often a sad, sentimental day for the farming family concerned, to see their worldly assets go under the hammer including 'Mother's' favourite cow, it is also a 'day out' for a large crowd of country folk. They arrive early, wander round, not only to inspect livestock, implements and the miscellaneous items on offer but to snoop around the buildings and the milking parlour. "See what sort of a set-up he's got here, we might learn some'mat, although from what I've seen driving past on the main road I should say its doubtful, all behind the times if you ask me." This would be the likely answer if one asked a local. Perhaps some fifty percent of the crowd have only come for a respite from their own labours with scant intention of buying anything. Most of the others will only purchase if they see a bargain, leaving a minority who have marked a particular item in the sale catalogue to buy at almost any price. The incoming tenant often gives the auctioneer written buying instructions or gets a friend to bid on his behalf, after all certain lots could be worth more to him since there is no transport involved. The majority of farm disposal sales take place in the autumn, Michaelmas, the end of the farming year. However, the odd one in the spring or anytime in the year, for that matter, draws a large crowd even if its a pouring wet day or six inches of snow covers the frozen ground!

Two of the village lads, having absconded from school try to organise the motorised vehicles. "Lorries on that side of the field please, cars to the right. I know its wet on that side, don't worry sir, we've got a tractor to pull you out if you get bogged down." Most of the motor manufacturers are represented, from the expensive

Jaguars, BMWs, Volvo and Range Rovers of the more wealthy farming community, to the battered 'other makes' towing a small trailer. The mud-splattered Land Rover with a collie sheep dog in the back. The twenty-year old banger with evidence of calf transport on the rear seat. Tractors and trailers with the driver set on loading any purchase as soon as possible. Flat lorries with mechanical hoist from 'over the bridge'. Always a fair attendance of Welshmen at farm sales. Now come a cattle wagon or two driven by such well-known characters as Gordon Sheerman, Mr Breakspear, Miss King and of course myself. One cast one's eyes down the rows of parked vehicles. Knowing some of their owners one could estimate the strength of the opposition at the days gathering.

10 a.m. On the far side of the meadow someone is ringing a large hand bell. Time for the auction to commence. Dreweatt, Watson and Barton are conducting this sale, so Desmond Barton will be selling. Last week John Pallett sold for A W Neate & Son. Next farm sale which is near Reading it will be Dick Long or Lindsay MacKay. All experienced auctioneers with the ability to put the crowd in a jovial mood with spirited bidding.

The auctioneer makes a brief speech. "Now you all know the reason for calling this sale? The owner is giving up his tenancy, planning to retire and live on his hard-earned savings." Laughter all round as few of those present really believe any tenant farmer has money in the bank! "He has farmed here all his life having taken over on his father's death so you've got two generations of farm tackle, something to suit everybody. The tractors, implements and farm machinery are all well maintained despite the age of some of it. The livestock will be sold 'right and straight' you've got one hour, after the fall of the hammer to complain of any faults. All the deadstock is sold 'as seen' so don't come back afterwards and tell me there is a nut missing or a wheel is buckled on your bargain of the day. There is a wooden shed adjoining the big barn, you may get your sale ticket there. Please pay for any purchase you make today, I don't wish to go round knocking on your back door asking for money. Later on we have a few pigs to offer, don't forget a movement licence is required before any pig leaves the farm, the local policeman will be in attendance for that job this afternoon. Finally, please make sure you take your correct lots, you may look a handsome, honest crowd of chaps but things do vanish at farm sales and

Hoping for a bargain

I would remind you that its yours at the fall of the hammer. Now I'm not going to give any more advice, I've got to talk all day so lets get started, bid up, we've got a lot to get through."

It is an interesting and rewarding experience to stand back on the sideline and cast one's eye over the crowd surrounding the auction-eer and his clerk. They are a cast unto themselves, decent, hard-working country folk all trying in their various ways to wrest a living from the land, not an easy task and one that seems to get more difficult as the years pass. First look around the sea of heads, one will observe a wide variety of head-gear with flat caps in the major-ity, others with storm-tossed hair blowing in the wind, a few display a sun-tanned bald patch. Weatherworn they lean on fork thumb-sticks, stand around deep in conversation with an acquaintance often only met at such events. Dressed in grease covered overalls, wellworn jackets, or waterproofs, most will be wearing wellies or stout boots to cope with the usual muddy conditions. The few ladies present look smart in their barbours and hunter boots.

The deadstock items for sale all have lot numbers and are spaced out in straight lines across the home meadow. Certain specific lots such as mills, grinders, mixers, fuel tanks, garden shed, etc will be offered in situ. The purchaser given time to dismantle and remove.

Lot 1. Invariably a large heap of scrap iron attracts the attention of local 're-cycling merchants' as they like to be called these days. "What am I bid for this lot, must weigh at least five tons" says the auctioneer. "Come on, start the ball rolling, fifty pounds surely? "Tenner" says my old school mate, Gordon Passey. He buys at thirty pounds. More money is made from other people's discarded rubbish than one would imagine. The auctioneer strives to maintain momentum as he moves down the line getting a laugh or two at the expense of some unique character whom he knows can take a joke. Buyers will part with their money more freely if kept in a jovial mood, the sun shines, and they can outbid a rival.

"Now then you chaps. Lot 24. Two chicken houses on wheels, well, they are on wheels but there is no guarantee that they will move far." All they need is a coat of creosote and someone handy with hammer and nails, nows the time to get back into free-range hens, sell the eggs at the door, the missus will make a small fortune." No-one believes him, they are knocked down at £10 the pair to a little man with a limp.

Lot 30. "Now, something unusual, a flight of stairs, made in oak too, and just look at the length of them, reach halfway to heaven these would, that will be nearer than most of you lot will ever get." Plenty of boisterous laughter greets that one. Like most of the other lots the stairs found a buyer, but there had been little competition for the chance to get halfway to paradise!

Next some iron pig troughs, always useful if only to fill with soil and plant a few flowers. Heaps of used timber, a large quantity of corrugated galvanised sheets in various lengths, work bench with vice, cow chains, garden tools, an anvil, grandad's two old scythes and his pitchfork. And so on down the line.

A pair of seventeen gallon milk churns with highly polished brass name plates make over two hundred pounds. "Man that bought them must be mad" says a voice behind me,

Prices are warming up, they are getting to the antique section, an Albion binder makes more than it cost new fifty years ago, a horse drawn mower, a Berkshire wagon, an old-fashioned seed drill, a shandy barrow, horse harness all meet competitive bidding. Much of this section will end up fully restored to its original state, with pride of place in some farm museum of rural life or our local show.

Time is marching on, another auctioneer takes over to give

Desmond a break before he sells the livestock. 'Modern' tackle now. Grass mower, fertilizer spinner, chemical sprayer, Cambridge roller, the disc harrows, maybe only half their original diameter find a Welsh buyer, as does the petrol driven Fergie and the Massey-Ferguson 135, they like small tackle on the mountain slopes!

The old pick-up baler and an ancient combine harvester attracts little interest. "Only used on this farm and both in working order I'm informed", states the auctioneer desperately trying to draw a bid. Approaching the end of the last line, the crowd has dispersed, some going to inspect the livestock, others drift towards a two wheeled caravan, with one side opened up it serves as a makeshift canteen. We pause for refreshments and two buxsom ladies, hard pressed to keep up with demand, serve hot steak and kidney pies, sausage rolls, cheese and pickle sandwiches and jam doughnuts. Weak tea and a dark brown liquid called coffee is poured into white plastic cups. "Help yourselves to sugar love, next please."

"Just a few lots of surplus furniture then a short break before we sell the livestock" announces the auctioneer. Household chattels attract little attention and even fewer bids. The kitchen table and four well-worn chairs, a sideboard, chest of drawers, and a cracked chamber pot with a glossy floral design. A collection of old prints and watercolours is being carefully scrutinised by a middle-aged lady who appears to know what she is looking for. "Come on, you bargain hunters, what am I bid for this lot? Double bed, complete with headboard and mattress, a sofa and two armchairs, oh, and the wardrobe. Put the lot together, get the job done." Silence, not a spark of interest from the sullen group. "Say something, one of you, fifty for the lot?" "Do you mean pence governor?" asks a black-bearded gent from the rear. "Come on, who'll start me off at £20" pleads the auctioneer. "Give you ten" says a voice. "Well, one bidder is worth a dozen onlookers I suppose. Any advance, if not it goes for a tenner, I've no reserve price. There you are young man, furnish your house with that little lot, all you need now is a wife."

The herd of thirty-two cross-bred milk cows, a few calves, some young stirks, a working horse, a pony, six saddleback sows, a large white boar and their progeny, fifty or so laying hens, and the Christmas geese make up the livestock section. A group of four or five prosperous looking gents stand in the corner of the big barn. They are the dealers who will take most of the cattle at the end of the day. If one could listen in on the conversation it would probably go like this. "Now, there is no point in us going hammer and tongs at each other, there is no-one here much interested in the cattle besides ourselves, so keep your eye on one another, don't take the other fella out, we can "knock-um out" at the end of the sale, that way there will be a good living for all of us." What was meant of course was that they would conduct a private auction between themselves at the end of the day. Untaxed, ready money would change hands, with the poor farmer on the losing side. All very illegal of course but a practice which happens every day at auction sales. The auctioneer turns a blind eye to such activity, he has got to get the stock sold, he dare not upset his main buyers, after all he will meet them all again at the weekly market.

The autumn sun sinks low in the west, it is getting quite late in the day before the hammer falls for the last time. Most of the deadstock paid for and loaded, a few small lots will hang around for a day or two, some may never get cleared.

The auctioneers and their clerks tot up the proceeds of the sale and make their way to the warmth of the farmhouse for a drop of the hard stuff. "Not a bad day on the whole governor considering the general shortage of money in the farming industry, and the fact that your deadstock was, well, to put it bluntly, rather antiquated. Cattle sold well too, taking into account there is little keep about, and we have a run of farm sales this autumn. We will get our cheque off to you in about a week's time. Should be a tidy sum to bank for your retirement.

In reality they know that there will be precious little left after deductions for advertising the sale, their commission charges, and the vendor has settle up all his outstanding bills, including the half-yearly rent due at the end of the month.

Such is the life and demise of the small tenant farmer.

Extracts from my farming diaries 1964 - 1975

I have always been completely happy and contented in my work, finding no toil or drudgery in it, experiencing a feeling of divine vocation in doing anything in connection with farming.

It is inevitable that throughout a farming year there will be many incidents, some sad, some tragic, mostly unavoidable, yet a few could have been avoided with greater care. One can find a certain amount of amusement in our misfortunes long afterwards, but at the time these catastrophes were certainly no laughing matter. Of course the happy, carefree days out-did the unhappy ones, if they hadn't I would long since have left the farming industry.

1964 January 15

Dora milked cows today unaided. Her understudy Dennis Hart had received an urgent telephone message from myself to drive to Newbury Livestock Market, load four calves and take them to the Isle of Wight in my mother's car!! "You sure that'll be alright, they'll make an awful mess in Grandma's car and I don't think there will be room for 'em" he queried. "Course it will be alright, they are only baby calves, bring four 'West of England' sacks, we will put them in bags and tie the mouth of the sack around their necks. If they dung it will not come through on the seat" I countered. Dismissing the fact that wee certainly would! Unfortunately Dennis got away to a late start. Car battery too flat to turn engine over in frosty weather. He had to get tractor and jump leads which all takes time.

Note:- Dennis Hart, a farmer's son from Keevil, had now joined the staff assisting with the milking and general farm work. His Wiltshire dialect was so pronounced that for some time we all had great difficulty in understanding him.

January 17

Dennis and myself repairing fence at the cemetery end of the

'Meadows'. His knowledge of this type of work seems to be almost nil. He explained to me that on his father's small council holding the fields were enclosed by quickthorn hedges and any gaps in them were repaired by the simple method of tying in place a hurdle or even part of an old iron bedstead!

January 18
Sixty-four 'West of England' sacks of malting barley sold and delivered to 'Allsops of Reading'.

January 26
My son Tony and Dennis set up new milking time record, putting 52 cows through parlour-adaptor in 45 minutes. Dennis' explanation for speed of through-put. "We gave 'um the beans today, didn't we Toe?"

January 27
The new Massey-Ferguson 135 tractor and three-furrow hydraulic plough delivered today. Admiration of this set-up from most of the family, all considered they are old enough to drive and from what I can gather, this even seems to include five year olds of either sex!

January 29
Two jobbing builders from Curridge gave me an estimate of £163 to cover repairs to the big barn at Red Farm. For this sum they will provide all materials required, mainly concrete blocks, timber and roofing tiles. They are hard working, reliable chaps so I think I will accept their price. I don't wish to see such a lovely historic building collapse for want of attention on my part.

February 2
Sunday, Mr Paulin came to plan the lay-out for new parlour following the demolition of bull pen.

February 13
Took delivery of new stainless steel bulk milk tank from 'Fullwoods'. However do these firms justify such high prices?

March 18
4.50 p.m. Milked cows in new parlour – what a shambles! Took four of us 2½ hours. Just eight gallons of milk in our 200 gallon tank – certainly not worth getting it dirty!

April 15
'Hills of Swindon' started on the task of erecting new covered yard for milk cows. This fine steel and asbestos clad building will house our herd in straw bedded luxury next winter. No more will the poor beasts have to sleep out in howling, rain-driven gales the whole night through.

May 3
Production of milk reached 100 gallons for the first time. Cows have now lost their prejudice of the new parlour. All in favour.

May 9
My 43rd birthday. Dora milked and broke milk production record set up by Dennis six days ago. 101 gallons in the tank. Keen competition amongst staff seems desirable!

August 9
Milk production has risen swifty through the summer months. Today the dipstick registered 184 gallons. Bulk tank a good investment after all.

October 27
Dennis trimming the roadside quickthorn hedge. Unfortunately a sharp thorn pierced his right eye. My wife and I rushed him to hospital. An anxious few hours followed, but after operation the verdict was favourable. Eyesight will be o.k.

November 3

Man called from Ministry of Agriculture. Information required regarding number of laying hens on the farm and their daily egg production. I was not available at the time. My overworked wife told-him that with seven children and a husband to feed and clothe, she didn't have time for such tom-foolery, but he was welcome to count the free-range hens himself if he wished!

November 8

Decision taken after talks with staff and family that the time had come to cold brand our cows with a number and year letter. No longer could we continue to remember all their names as the herd continued to expand, but it was mutually agreed that some of the old favourites, whilst having a number on their hindquarters would still respond to names. Names of long standing like, Dalmation Daisy, Topnotch, Dahlia, Grasshopper, Polka-Dot, Duchess, Lady Fawsley, Rosebud, Lollipop, Nanny Goat, Pitchfork, Cowslip, Wickham's Wonder, Rasher, Watch-it, Lightening and the inevitable Fillpail.

December 17

Laboriously prepared and presented a fat beast, a pen of porkers and a fat sow at Newbury Fat Stock Show. Sow took third prize and sold for £30.

December 21

Dennis and I finished pulling the last of the swedes, a cold, wet, miserable task. Perhaps we will enjoy our Christmas dinner now that job is behind us.

December 25

I had the 'pleasure' of milking the cows on the Lord's Birthday. The next day Tony helped me. Temperature never above zero. Cold hands and frozen feet in the cowshed make the evening in front of our huge log fire something to look forward to.

1965

January is a tough month, an uphill climb to the warmth of spring and those people who have time for holidays are busy saving up for the summer vacation. For us country yokels who have chosen a farm career we must continue to act as midwife to our bovine charges in the dead of night, thaw out frozen cattle troughs and splash through ankle-deep mud to feed outlying stock.

January 15

Received telephone call from a Mr Napper, an elderly smallholder who lived in the village of Blewbury on the edge of the Berkshire Downs. He had been told that I purchased cattle. "Yes" I replied, but spring grass is a long way off." However I told him I would drive over to see what he had for sale. The sight that met my eyes on arrival was one that I will never forget. I almost fell over laughing. In a small barn in the last stages of delapidation, four sad-eyed shorthorn steers gazed down at their owner and myself. This building had obviously been their abode for quite a long period of time, in fact I was to learn that they had been placed there as baby calves. By now the accumulation of straw and manure was so deep that the anaemic looking, long horned store cattle upon it had long since eaten all the thatched roof and there they stood with heads through the rafters?

Needless to say we struck a deal, I could never resist a bargain, experience told me that with summer grass these big-boned animals would be top beef by autumn. That was all very well, but the immediate problem was how to get them into the cattle truck. There was no point in opening the barn door, the dung was too high. We had to dismantle part of the roof timbers but of course, even though we placed bales of straw on the outside no amount of pushing, shoving or coaxing would move those beasts from the security of their home. Finally Mr Napper lassoed each in turn, pulling them off their perch with a tractor as they plunged and bellowed in protest.

February 11

I made enquiries about the purchase of a new fore-loader for the Ferguson tractor. The cheapest price I could get was £110. With more and more farmyard manure each year more mechanisation had to come. Our four-grained prongs must soon be museum pieces.

Feb 13

"Dahlia", always a greedy cow, tried to get more than her fair share of silage and got stuck between the metal silage barrier and the railway sleeper wall. Pulled her out with a tractor and a long hessian rope – no permanent injury except a nasty graze on her back.

Feb 22

Delivery taken today of new Welgar hay and straw baler. More machinery, more production, less men, the only way forward we are constantly told by the experts.

"Great interferers" I call them. Government agencies and pressure groups led by well-meaning, muddle-headed people who are not country men and find it hard to understand the process of nature. Yet, perhaps I'm the one that is wrong. If you live in one place long enough you become glued to the same hill, like an old sheep.

February 24

What a day, I honestly don't remember such a wet spell as we have had these last two weeks and today capped the lot. One consolation is that no matter how much rain the clouds throw at us, Mousefield Farm, perched high on the hillside, will never get flooded. I do not care for winter at all – most winters in my opinion are too long, bringing wailing wind, driving rain, and ferocious snow blizzards from the north. Every time you get a bad one as in 1947 or '63, it takes something away from you in the physical sense, whatever your age or physical condition. The animals need foddering every day, so out you go, whether or not there's a storm brewing. Mind you, the old fashioned, strong hessian sack is wonderful for keeping you warm and dry. I always sported three sacks – one around my waist, another over the shoulders, and the third with the corners pushed in for a hood over my head.

February 26

Sign of the times. Purchased a pedigree Friesian stock bull from Mr Wickham for the sum of £100.

March 13, 2.30 a.m.
Ada gave birth to a huge bull calf. My eldest son Michael assisted. "Why do the majority of our cows have to go into labour in the early hours?" When sensible people are enjoying a well earned sleep, we find ourselves hanging on to the end of calving ropes in the middle of the night!

April 9
We have always had mud but this year caps the lot. 'Wild eyes' always a silly bitch, heavy with calf, got herself well and truly stuck up to her belly in the boggiest corner of the 'Runways'. She was successfully lassoed and dragged free with 'Teddie' the Standard Fordson. Unfortunately when clear of the quagmire she was too weak to stand. Called Vet, he diagnosed cracked knee cap, may take six weeks to recover.

April 16
'Wild eyes' stood up today, though still very wobbily on her pins. She has responded well to patient nursing. We are all more hopeful of her making a full recovery,

April 21
Divided cow grazing fields into twenty-one, two acre paddocks with electric fencing. The plan is to give the herd a different block each day. It will of course take twenty-one days to rotate, thus the herd will have fresh, green, untrodden grass each day.

April 23
A sad day. Despite optimistic hopes 'Wild eyes' never fully recovered. Today she was shot and ignominiously dragged by a chain attached to her hind leg, slowly up the ramp of a lorry to be transported to the knacker's yard. Her flesh for dog and cat food, her hide for leather boots, shoes and ladies handbags, and her bones processed into fertilizer for the garden.
There is an old saying in the farming world. "If you keep livestock sure enough you will have deadstock."

April 24
Pounds Field. Recently ploughed for the first time in living memory this desperately dry, sandy field of just one acre was drilled with Procter barley and undersown with 34 lbs rye grass. With luck and summer rain we may harvest one and a half tons of grain! A pitiful amount by English standards but a year's rations for a few of the world's starving.

May 4
A wet day spent weighing off sacks of wheat in the big barn at Red Farm. Total ready for sale. 136 West of England sacks at 1½ cwt each.

May 18
Purchased for the sum of thirty-three pounds, one ton of fertilizer from Berks, Bucks & Oxon Farmers Ltd. My wife accused me of wanton extravagance. "What is wrong with our large stock of farm-yard manure?" she demanded.

June 5
Saturday. A warm, pleasant, summer's day, a joy to be alive until two strong town dogs panicked twenty-five yearling beef calves through the roadside hedge. Dora, some of the kids and myself had a right rodeo rounding them up. Dora got knocked over and trampled underfoot. The air was blue for the next few minutes but fortunately no harm done.

June 24
Our ewe flock is now depleted to twenty head. Alec Adnams sheared them today in the big barn.

June 25
One of the newly sheared ewes died today. No doubt from shock, a sheep hasn't got much will to live. At least we have the fleece!

July 25
Dennis milked cows today, also put on tell-tale tags. Different coloured one-inch wide bands on their tails inform us at a glance their approximate calving dates and other details. He reported trou-

ble with cows at milking time. They were very restless, swishing their tails, swinging their heads, kicked off the milking clusters and constantly dunged over everything. The muggy thundery weather caused the flies to be very active. Request for me to call in the "Fly Killing Man" with his spray gun.

August 1
Making hay on the 'Island'. This seven acre island is created by a bend in the River Kennet and the Avon and Kennet Canal east of Newbury. 'Betsy' the Fergie tractor caught fire also some of the crop went up in flames. Maybe our punishment for working on a Sunday. Luckily plenty of water nearby.

August 5
Grain harvest for us has commenced. Got off to a bad start. Dennis and myself on bagger combine in field at Stable Farm. Went ten yards-threshing drum blocked. By the end of the day we had circled the field just six times. At this rate it would be quicker to get out the old binder and go back to rick building!

August 9
Weather extremely dry, very short of water. Extracted three hundred gallons from River Lambourn. Transported on a trailer in milk churns to water cattle in 'High Wood' meadow.

August 19
Bluebottle', a favourite cow seemed very distressed this morning. I'm sure she has had a calf in the night but no sign of her offspring. "Come on Bluebottle, where's your baby, you got one hidden away somewhere I feel sure." Lowing gently she lead me to the highest point of the 'Runways' an isolated spot and there was a pretty heifer calf just a few hours old with its front legs hopelessly entangled in wire netting erected to keep rabbits at bay.

August 20
All the family helped clear sacks of wheat after combining finished for the day. Worked until one a.m. by the feeble light given off by a Tilly Lamp.

September 15
Harvest finished at last. Its been difficult and expensive due to inclement weather this season. Promised family a day in London tomorrow. "Is that a reward or a punishment?" someone asked.

October 22
Police call at farm. Report Friesian heifers straying on the B4009 in thick fog. Investigation proves they are indeed ours, some rambler had left a roadside gate open.

1966 March 8
Woke to a bone chilling north wind. Ground frozen, thick ice on water troughs. Cows don't like this weather, milk production has dropped alarmingly. March has certainly come in like a lion. Must pin our hopes on it going out like the traditional lamb.
'Betsy' the Fergie returned. Fire damage now made good by South Berks Engineering Co at a cost of £100.

June 26
All available members of our family and two collie dogs assist in driving large herd of cattle from the 'Island' back to the home farm. Chaos caused on A4. Proved a fact I had known for a long time – cars and livestock don't mix!

July 17
This year I took our small flock of sheep to a shepherd near Basingstoke to have them sheared at a cost of two shillings and six-pence each (12½p). Easier than doing the job myself and ending up with a bad back for a month!

August 21
Dora, Tony, Stephen and Mum standing up straw bales in small stacks. A thankless job, but it does give bales some protection against wet weather.

August 23
Combining wheat at Cold Ash Farm for Mr Talmage. Combine caught fire. Flames put out by quick use of fire extinguisher. No serious damage done.

October 31

Guernsey cow got her head wedged between two posts in railway fence. Called British Rail. Man on the other end of telephone said. "We have more than enough worry keeping trains running without rescuing stupid cows." Solved problem myself by sawing down railway fence.

December 14

Plumber employed by Arthur A Beaver, Heating Engineers from Heath End, East Woodhay arrived this morning and started on the task of fixing oil-fired central heating system in Mousefield Farm House. Hopefully all should be working before Christmas. No longer will we all freeze when we move away from the log fire! It was whilst 'helping' this workman as a five year old that my youngest son, Stephen, acquired the nickname Fred which was to stick with him for the rest of his life.

1967 August 30

Harvest going well until today. Wheat was flowing into the grain trailer at a fair crack when without warning the overheated six cylinder engine exploded with an almighty bang. Sure scared the life out of me. Luckily the resulting fire was rapidly brought under control by the prompt use of fire extinguisher carried on board.

September 1

Oakes Bros Ltd fitted reconditioned engine into combine harvester. Full marks for an efficient service to a farmer in dire need.

November 14

Wife in mad rush to town for spare parts drove car into deep roadside ditch. No injury, but car bodywork not improved. Dennis our man of many skills pulled car out with tractor and tow rope.

1968 January I

First day of the New Year. Got off to a bad start I must say. Beef cattle escaped from yard. Fugitives took off unnoticed down farm drive making for town, collecting reinforcements from another farmer's field en route. Finally stopped by Police and public at Shaw Mill, just a few hundred yards short of the notorious Robin Hood roundabout.

January 6
Mousefield Farm Gymkhana. Days of preparation getting jumps and obstacle course ready paid off. All our children's school friends who own a horse or pony came along, great fun was had by all.

January 15
Kathleen (better known these days as A 152) one of our best cows collapsed with severe milk fever. Despite all our efforts and massive intravenous injections of calcium, she died in the afternoon.

March 14
Demo organised by South Berks Engineering Co. Four-wheel drive Zetor tractor.

March 17
Typical March gale today. Workshop roof almost blown off. Daughter Jane roped it down single-handed until help arrived. In the medley to save the roof Tim ran over his mother's leg with the Land Rover, no bones broken.

March 18
Livestock dealer Stewart Trotman came to farm with a "cheap" cow. He claimed she was an excellent milker with a high butter-fat percentage. Like motor car salesmen, cattle dealers point out the good points of their wares conveniently forgetting the bad ones. Purchased cow for £65. Dora took an instant dislike to the new cow and for some reason promptly named her "Frying Pan".

April 12
Manure spreader broke down. At this rate we will not get our great heaps of muck onto the field in time to plant kale. 'Betsy's' batteries not charging. Discovered that the leads were connected back to front.

June 24
Harvesting silage from Big Easton. Relief tractor driver hit a tree. Some damage to new Zetor tractor.

December 5
Lorry from the Midlands driven into roadside hedge at the meadows. Twenty yards of quickthorn and wide ditch obliterated. Took driver to hospital with broken arm and shock.

1969 January 22
Calf born with twisted gut. A pretty heifer calf from a good cow. It had no future, taken to slaughter house. It will become ingredients for veal and ham pies.

February 26
Two unkempt characters called, driving an ancient Ford flat truck. They were selling cheap iron farm gates. Sent them packing.

March 6
Shorthorn cow called Duchess that had been retained in the yard for Artificial Insemination fell into slurry tank. Only her head showing above foul smelling liquid. Called Fire Brigade, R.S.P.C.A. came as well. Right old caper; we had to rescue her. "The downfall of a Duchess" was the headline in our local paper.

April 2
N.A.A.S. man came today. He suggested change of farming policy to overcome drastic fall in our profits. Cut out corn growing, establish second dairy herd at Red Farm (our land on opposite side of the valley), milking them through an open air bale system. May be sound in theory but I pointed out to him that these days it is almost impossible to get a cowman willing to milk cows in the open in all weathers.

April 28
Typical day. Grinding mill broke down. Cows got out onto main road, puncture in trailer tyre. ' Bob' the new Zeter tractor refused to start. Otherwise, everything fine including the weather.

July 12
Called Vet to sick calves. They had been housed at Dymond Farm in the old tin cowshed with green painted doors. Vet diagnosed lead poisoning caused by calves licking old paint. One calf died, three

more seriously ill. Survivors circle endlessly to the right with damaged brains. Doors now dismantled. Liken to closing the stable door after the horse has bolted!

July 21
John Simcock (cowman), Tony, Richard and Fred overhauled both combine harvesters. All set for harvest soon as weather settled.

August 18
Still using bagger combine. Total of 940½ cwt sacks of barley from 'Redland' field. 31 cwts to the acre. 2300 bales of straw to be moved manually!

August 28
Combine kept breaking down. Fan belt broke, leak in radiator, must continuously top-up water cooling system. Tim baling straw until string box fell off baler.

September 4
Combining barley at Stable Farm. The last field this season. On second time round crop there was an almighty racket. We had picked up an old pram someone had thrown into our standing corn and it had got into the works. Took rest of the afternoon to remove mangled metal from combine's innards. Some damage done to beater bars.

September 16
Cow gave birth to twins whilst herd grazed the 'Runways'. One calf vanished. Dora, John, Tim, Richard, Mum and myself searched without success. "How do you know there are twin calves Dora?" I enquired. "Cos I seed two with me own eyes of course, when I got tud'ther cows in for milking" says Dora crossly.

September 19
Dora found second calf alive and well in the depth of Mousefield Copse. Hidden in the bracken having survived three days without food or drink.

September 23
Ordered 300 gallon bulk milk tank to cope with expected autumn production.

October 20
Tim ploughed up an old rusty cash box at Red Farm. Thoughts of a fortune in golden sovereigns evaporated on forcing open locked lid, empty.

October 26
Houghton Family V Didcot Wonders. Football match played on home ground at Mousefield Farm. We lost 4 – 1. Small wonder I played goal keeper and I'm not a 'diver' between the posts.

December 5
Student Austin and myself drove lorry to Longleat Estate where I purchased 500 pressure-treated fencing posts for £95.

1970 April 7
Cows out to grass today, one month early. Just as well because hay and silage all eaten.

April 12
Spring is in the air. Primroses have been in blossom for a month, Bluebells almost at their best. Oaks coming into leaf. Family cleaning and repairing their bicycles.

April 20
Moved cattle to meadows on main road. A car driver approached herd driving too fast, braked hard, lost control and turned his car over onto its roof. We helped him out of his car through open window. Shaken but otherwise unhurt, he said "Didn't see your cows until too late to stop." "What, didn't notice sixty big Friesian cows walking down a straight road in broad daylight?" I asked in amazement.

April 23
John Simcox fertilized five cow grazing paddocks in pumping meadow. Used one ton ICI No. 2.

May 12
John, Dora and myself cold branded cows. Kept branding irons in dry ice. Hold branding iron required on cows flank for 30 seconds. No pain to cow. No marks noticeable today, however we are told that in two or three weeks time the black hairs of the cow where iron was held will turn white exposing the number or letter required for identification.

June 4
John Simcox milked our cows for the last time. He is leaving the industry for more money and a five day week with a security firm.

June 23
I sprayed Red Farm Downs with Phenoxoline. Charlie Walter our new cowman started work.

July 8
Tony fixed up cow pegboard. A very well thought out method of moving coloured pegs to keep the dairy herd statistics.

July 15
Tony, Tim and Mike Hogan erecting grain silo. A Heath-Robinson affair consisting of an upright wire cylinder, inside a large black rubber bag to hold grain. Rats are reputed to ignore contents because they cannot smell food. Time will tell!

July 29
Tim cultivating ploughed ground in Railway Fields. Not finished, tractor jammed in low gear.

August 4
Tony planted grass seed. Job not finished, he smashed up seed box – took all day to repair.

September 15
Ten tons No. 2 Fertilizer and ten tons Nitram delivered. Seems like the more fertilizer one uses the more is required each year. Gone are the days when I purchased 'the stuff in blue bags' one ton at a time!

October 16

Back into sheep once more. Purchased 100 store lambs at Wilton Sheep Fair. Hopefully they will eat off our surplus autumn grass and return a useful profit early in the new year when sold as fat hoggets.

October 22

Tim and Charlie Walters double fencing our boundary. Our herd now brucellosis free which means they must have no physical contact with our neighbour's cattle whose stock is untested and could be carrying the disease.

October 31

I purchased three cows from the Duke of Westminster. He is reputed to be England's richest man but his agent still wanted top price for the cattle.

November 9

Away to an early start. I drove my cattle wagon to Five Lanes Market Launceston, Cornwall. My friend Bimbo Payne and his son, Richard came too. A bit cramped in the cab on such a long journey. The first Autumn Sale of suckled calves would take place next day. We stayed overnight in a B & B at £4.50 per head.

November 10

Purchased 27 suckled calves.

November 11

Sow which had given birth to thirteen piglets whilst running wild in Easton Copse, cannot be found reported Dora, who has been feeding the family every day. Eventually found at Mr Anderson's farm in Ashmore Green. Dora and the cowman sent to get them back home again. Failed in their attempt. Report sow too fierce, repeatedly charged them open-mouthed.

Tim and myself succeeded just before dark. Sow and piglets now confined to piggery under lock and key.

November 30

Charlie, Tim and myself building slurry ramp. Grand opening planned for Christmas. We will then be able to push cow slurry up the ramp with tractor fitted yard scraper direct into muck spreader. Much more efficient then the laborious broom and shovel method!

December 25
Cow number seventy died in calf-birth. Not a pleasant Christmas Box!

1971 February 19
Official called from Ministry of Agriculture re calf subsidy for beef calves aged between nine months and one year. He passed thirteen out of sixteen presented. Punching a small round hole in each of the calves right ear which had qualified. By this method the farmer is prevented from claiming subsidy twice. The three were rejected for subsidy because the man from the Ministry after looking in their mouths noticed that these calves had cut two broad teeth, having lost two of their baby teeth. He believed them to be older than one year. "Perhaps I had got their birth dates wrong?" he said. I suggested "he should ignore the small matter of the size of a calf's tooth. After all, if I called him in everytime my calves reached nine months of age he could be making six visits to my farm each year instead of two. Think of the extra expense in petrol and demands on his valuable time." But no, I lost my subsidy money on the three rejects. "Rules are there to be followed" he tactfully explained.

March 20
Daughter Jane harrowing front paddocks after school. She is quite a useful tractor driver these days.

March 23
Hereford Bull got out again. He has got fifty wives, seems he is never satisfied. Caught amongst neighbour's maiden heifers. Best to keep quiet, perhaps no harm done. Will hear in due course if neighbour's heifers drop calves with white faces!

March 30
Have now run out of hay and silage for the dairy cows. No grass to graze yet, and the wind continues to blow from the north. Cows grazing rye. This cereal grows well at lower temperatures and it has certainly been our salvation this spring.

May 2
Dora milked and production exceeded 200 gallons for the first time. Must consider Dora for a bonus.

May 18
On the way to Salisbury Cattle Market I picked up a young lady hitch-hiker, Linda Smith, a farmer's daughter from Alberta, Canada, and made a friend for life.

June 21
Tony planted railway fields with thousand-headed kale.

June 23
Mum and the gang stood up hay bales. 300 at Red Farm and 300 at Mousefield Farm. All workers in a state of collapse at end of the day.

July 5
Hay has stood out in the field for two weeks, now well dried out. All worked until midnight getting hay bales into barn. Winter cow rations now secure.

July 7
Son Tony off to work in New Zealand. We shall miss his help on this farm.

July 19
Everyone called out to rogue wild oats in eighteen acres. Dora moaned a lot. "Can't stand the blessed job, traipse up and down the rows of corn looking for them weeds, pulling them up and carrying them to the headland to stack in heaps ready for burning. Can't you afford to buy some 'oh that chemical to kill 'em off like other farms be doing these days?"

July 25
Started work on erecting a farm worker's bungalow at the entrance to Red Farm. Digging foundations in the chalk subsoil with pick and shovel. Tim, Charlie, Dora, Jane, Cousin Sue Baker, Richard, Fred, Mother, Self and Bobby now age seven years. A gang of ten unskilled but willing navies. Volunteers better than pressed

men anyday. When the work is finished and occupied by a farm worker I will collect £10 each year from the Newbury District Council for the next forty years. Something to look forward to.

August 24
Purchased a second-hand drill and a plough from Oakes Bros Ltd for £250.

August 25
Purchased a chisel plough from Bartrops. The reason behind this latest acquisition is to break up the hard pad of subsoil below the usual ploughing depth and to aerate the soil.

October 21
I am called for a month's duty at Quarter Sessions. Turned out to be a great experience in human problems but placed a great demand on my valuable time.

November 13
I took two of my sons, Tim and Fred on the train north to watch a football match. Manchester City against Derby County. Marvellous atmosphere, flat caps and northern accents much in evidence. A great match, pity Fred's team 'Manchester City' lost, one nil. We stood behind City's goalposts.

1972 March 3
Coach load of Oxford University Students came from the City of Spires to visit a working farm. I wonder how many have returned still with the desire to make a career on the land?

March 6
I went to the Paris Agricultural Show with Alan Shackleton and a party of farmers.

March 10
Commenced the erection of cow cubicle housing.

May 20
I repair tractor trailer. New floor, second-hand Russian Pine.

Billy Bean's Machine

June 29
Tony passed HGV test. Now we have two lorry drivers if needed.

August 7
Vet injected all milk cows and in-calf heifers with Tribovax.

August 20
Tony and Tim constructed 'Billy Bean's machine', a weird contraption made of a combine grain box, gears, levers and belts to clean and bag off grain.

September 28
Tony and Tim fixing Yorkshire Boarding on new beef unit at Dymond Farm.

November 23
Mum, Tim and self drove to High Wycombe to inspect a milking parlour. Most impressive.

December 30
Milking parlour experts drawing plans for our new parlour.

1973 January 19
The Juby family from New Zealand are staying with us – all seven of them. House at full capacity.

April 3
Ministry of Agriculture approved plans and grants available for our new parlour. Construction started immediately, all family working after school. A real team effort. Richard and Jane breaking up stones – convict work!

April 25
Will miss the help of two of our main construction workers, Tony back to Wye College. Richard returned to Kingswood College, Bath.

May 14
Tim moved parlour into place.

June 28
Tim ploughing kale ground, very dry and hard. Bent plough beam.

June 29
Mum, Dora, Tim and self milked cows through new parlour for the first time.

June 30
Tim drilled kale ground.

July 22
Combining winter barley. Heavy going, took five days to harvest 18 acres.

September 28
Tim off to Burchett's Green Agricultural College.

September 29

Tim came home again unexpected – ploughing Highwood field – no-one else can do it properly, he maintained.

1974 January 19

I fix new roof on our sun parlour in anticipation of sunny days to come!

March 28

Purchased a section of the Newbury – Didcot railway line which passes through our estate. Three and three-quarter acres for £375 (£100 per acre).

March 30

Commenced removing derelict railway fence ready for Jack Hatt, Agricultural contractors to reclaim land for agriculture after over one hundred years under steel rails and wooden sleepers.

August 25

Painted galvanised tin barn at Red Farm. All family helped, more red paint on painters than on building!

October 13

Jane had her first car driving lesson.

1975 January 17

A cold blustery winters day. Tim and myself getting straying heifers out of John Bennett's flower garden. Why do cattle have to dance with glee when they trespass? Repairs needed to boundary fence please note.

March 25

More progress. Farmplan cow kennels delivered. Each wooden section cut to size.

May 30

Ida, (one of the old cows still referred to by name) blown on spring clover grass. Unfortunately died despite prompt treatment by Vet.

June 2
Our elm trees show the first signs of Dutch Elm Disease. We were hoping they may have escaped this slow death.

July 8
Tim ridging potatoes in Railway fields.

July 17
Mum, Jane, Fred, Bobby and myself leave on camping tour holiday in Scotland including the Isle of Skye.

August 9
Richard spraying noxious weeds in alpine garden using knapsack sprayer.

September 1
Jane builds a greenhouse which we purchased for £99 from Scats.

September 8
Tim erecting six foot high security fence around slurry lagoon.

September 26
My wife purchased 50 laying hens and one cockerel at Mr Billy Wallace's farm sale. Price 25p each.

October 6
Dora cutting potato halm with her sickle.

October 8
On the way to the mill with a load of grain. Trailer tipped over with Dora on it. She landed in the middle of the busy B4009 amongst four tons of barley. Luckily no bones broken but air very blue!

October 9
Richard and myself drove cattle lorry to Banbury Market taking two barren cows. Blackie sold for £204 and an unnamed heifer for £238. First time any of our cows sold for meat over £200.

October 26

Spinning out spuds in railway field. The heaviest weighed 1lb 11 ozs.

November 12

Cutting frozen kale by hand sickle. Fed to milk cows. Unfortunately this green crop taints the milk and makes cows scour but desperately short of hay and silage this winter.

November 24

I drove wagon to Canterbury to collect rockery stones. Some weighed half a ton each. Giving priority to flower garden in preference to cows will never do, but if it makes for a happy marriage!

December 14

Egg production from new hen flock now averaging ten eggs per day. Not a great money spinner but very nice to have our own fresh eggs once again.

December 16

"Oh dear!" All milk went down the drain. I forgot to put plug in base of bulk tank!

December 18

Cows used new cubicles for first time. I'm afraid quite a few cows disapprove preferring to stand in the dung passage all night. Perhaps they will learn in time!!

December 22

Tim and Richard working on the construction of a new farm workshop. It will be a great advantage to have all farm tools and accessories under lock and key and in one place.

December 31

So ends yet another farming year. I wonder what 1976 will bring? We always hope and pray for good health for all the family, better prices, good crops, increases in milk yield, better weather with rain in some fields but not in others, disease-free stock, less disastrous events, and more profit at the end of another year's slog. But it is too much to expect all our prayers to be answered.

So you wish to be a Farmer?

Be warned, farming is no life for comfort lovers or softies, its a tough trade in the unforgiving world of the elements.

There is a 'farming ladder' for all who can make use of it, but remember it is a ladder and not an escalator, it must be climbed step by step and it can take a life-time. There will be a helping hand from some but beware there are many who would endeavour to push you off and although it may enable you to achieve the heights you may never reach the top. Given the will there is hardly anything which one cannot accomplish.

One important lesson to be learnt is that good farming is the cumulative effect of making the best possible use of one's land, labour and capital not to be confused with neat and tidy farming only, which is often uneconomic. Although I always endeavoured to keep my farm shipshape somehow I never quite got perfection. In farming for a living on a small family farm one is condemned to a life of unremitting toil, in mud, snow or dust: few holidays, no security, poverty and want, saving all the years for a set of false teeth and a coffin. The alternative is an occupation with security, promotion and a useful pension at the end of it.

My greatest asset was a wife with absolute faith in herself, her husband and her children, all seven were given the best education we could afford and a free choice of trade or profession but all would have to make their own way on leaving school or college.

For the would-be farmer male or female this is my advice on how to achieve your goal. First a good background education at an agricultural college and there are many excellent ones around. Next must come practical experience. Try a year on a dairy farm, another on an arable unit, finally perhaps yet one more year on a first class general farm which should include plenty of livestock, beef unit, a sheep flock, pigs or poultry. You must be conscientious, prepared to work hard and long hours and never forget, ask plenty of questions from your employer and other stockmen, why do you do this or that, why, why, why, you can never learn too much and read plenty of books on your subject.

If you really wish to be a farmer, 'don't buy a motor car', it is an unnecessary and very expensive piece of equipment to own whilst trying to reach that first step on the ladder. You can get around just as well on two sturdy legs, a bicycle or public transport. Save all the money you can even if it means living the life of a pauper. On days off work visit agricultural shows or the nearest livestock market, where you will learn the wiles and guiles of men who make their living from the land.

If you like livestock, don't mind an early start to the day, and fancy milking cows, set yourself up as a contract milker, you can earn good money and you will also get plenty of work. The next step is to find a farmer who has the land, a good herd of cows, a decent set-up and no son to carry on the business. By now you should have some money stacked away.

Share farming – the method first started in New Zealand – will pave the way for any enthusiastic young person to get a start. If you do enter farming this way do of course get a first class contract drawn up. With your youth and the influx of extra capital this should rejuvenate the business. Who knows, in a few more years your ageing farmer may wish to retire completely. He may even leave you the farm in his will!

Another method I rather admired. Whilst walking the vast open hills to the south-west of Newbury I chanced to meet a young man erecting a long length of electric sheep netting. Two well-trained collie dogs sat patiently in the rear of his Land Rover. In every direction as far as the eye could see stretched mile upon mile of almost uninhabited downland. He seemed pleased to meet another human being especially someone who was interested in his work. I was soon to learn that he was the proud owner of some two thousand breeding ewes and yet he didn't own an acre of land. The ewes and their lambs were all grazed on agisted keep. He moved them around the district mainly on arable farmers land, whom it seemed welcomed this man's sheep as a break crop on short rotation leys or stubble turnips. He explained to me that some ten years ago, whilst working on an arable farm as a tractor driver, his employer suggested that he could keep a few sheep as a perk if he wished. From the local market he purchased thirty-five old, broken-mouthed inlamb ewes. From the lamb crop he retained the best females, purchased a pedigree ram and from this small beginning slowly built up to his present numbers which was now more than a fulltime job. He had purchased a bungalow on the edge of the village and married a girl who proved to be a better shepherd than he was. He expressed the hope that one day he would purchase his own farm. I got the feeling that that day was not too distant.

If all else fails, don't despair, just marry a wealthy farmer's son or daughter, and don't be put off by pessimistic folk telling you that farming is finished. Not on your life, there are an awful lot of people around with the strong desire for a five day week and don't forget they all get hungry every day!

On with the Show

If farming is still the backbone of the country, then the agricultural shows are a multi-coloured cloak worn proudly over the broad shoulders of the farming community when, once a year, they take the country to the town. The essence of the show is people from the town coming out and joining their country cousins and having a fantastic time. Most of the shows are held in spring or autumn. The Newbury and Royal County of Berkshire Show comes at the end of a busy season on the third week-end in September, when the farmer and his loyal staff can relax for the first time with friends. You can't hold your head up at the show if you haven't finished the grain harvest. The spud lifting and maize cutting can wait, and there will be plenty of time for autumn cultivations and the seeding.

I have attended our local show from those far off days when I could walk under a working horse in the stable without ducking my head, following this annual event from one site to the next as it continued to outgrow itself. The year 1985 marked a further milestone in the show's continuous development, the first use of the Society's own showground after holding the event on other people's land for 75 years. This was a major step forward, since then the show has gone from strength to strength. My lifelong friend and associate, Roger Chapman was much involved in the negotiations to purchase the new site. He had the courage to see the future and to act accordingly. Sadly Lew Spencer, Secretary of the Show for many years, never lived to see the show take place on its new ground. Lew devoted long hours of hard work to ensure the success and popularity of the show. He was greatly missed. Stephen Burman (Chairman) Roger Chapman and Lew's life-long assistant, Beryl Fisher, continued to run the Show until Dr John Bines took over as the new Secretary.

One of the reasons for the financial success of the Show is the loyalty and unfailing support of its membership. So many members give freely of their time and expertise, stalwart supporters like Derek Smalley, the Showground Director and his assistants, Richard Liddiard and Chris Saint, backed up by Clem Cooper, David Rabbitts, Peter Carter and a complete army of helpers and advisers who generously loan tractors, implements and men, reseeding, fertilising and rolling. Work, that first year of occupation, ranged from fencing to roadways, from preparing adequate entrances, to levelling large holes in the field. Finally laying out the ground in a complete pattern of rings, stands, tents and tracking.

Mr Philip Wroughton of Woolley Park made a great impact as the Society's President that first year. He hosted pre-show activities such as the Wine and Cheese Party and the Sponsor's Lunch, which proved amongst the most successful in the Society's history. Generous sponsorship and prize money ensures that entry standards are of the highest quality.

I'd like to think that now the Society owns its own site it can put down permanent roots. It is a near perfect venue, although slightly undulating it is free draining and in a commanding position at the crossroads of England, the meeting point of the M4 and the A34 giving excellent access from afar. It will be a disaster if yet another road cuts across the land as some planners have suggested.

We should be celebrating – in a light hearted way – the survival of many rural skills and traditions despite all that has happened to dampen our spirits in the last ten years. A mere generation ago nearly everyone had an uncle, aunt, cousin or grandparent who worked or lived on a farm. That's no longer the case today, and as a result all the agricultural shows are very conscious of their economic survival. If the farmer's boat sinks it is not only the captain and crew who go down with the ship remember, it is everyone's food store as well! Town and country folk however still flock to our show, last year 1990, the attendance reached 73,000 – a record. It is one of the largest and best two-day shows in the country. The organisers have done a grand job but there is no room to be complacent we have all got to go into the 21st Century, taking a positive approach to entertainment.

For those folk who haven't yet enjoyed a day at our show let me have the pleasure of describing in my simple style what attractions, entertainments and amusements there are for the young and not so young. The multitudes who have visited this great annual event many times may like to be reminded of many happy hours spent at the greatest social occasion of the farming year. Everything is done on a grand scale with a picnic atmosphere, where there is still enough room in the car parks for people to cluster around their vehicles on arrival and refresh themselves with coffee and assorted goodies. More and more cars come streaming in, volunteer Young Farmers in white smocks with coloured armbands direct the traffic flow into regimental double lines. Everything is so well organised, Thames Valley Police should be highly commended for their part in what is truly a mammoth task controlling such a vast number of vehicles.

Crowds of people from coaches, cars and on foot flock to the entrance gate. Many like myself walk straight through proudly displaying our membership badge, some show their tickets purchased at reduced price prior to the day of the show, others fork out their money at the gate. All this entertainment for so many at no real cost to themselves, surely the bargain of the year?

For people used to the wonders of car telephones, fax machines, plastic cards and remote control the show offers riveting spectacles of earlier times. Here is a chance to see the farriers at work wielding seven pound hammers as they skillfully shape strips of red hot metal on the anvils making shoes to fit the heavy working horses waiting patiently nearby.

Beautifully restored steam engines drive authentic threshing machines of yesteryear. You will also see grinders, winnowers, water pumps, and sheep shearers at work. The show would be incomplete without Gordon and Philip Passey and all the other enthusiasts who proudly display their resplendent antique vehicles. Cars which date back to the earliest days of motoring. People should take the opportunity to sit down and enjoy a wide range of rural food, not just crass convenience food, like hot dogs and candy floss, but come and taste what we produce and quench their thirst at the flavoured milk stand.

Parents go with their children to look and admire the sheep, cattle and those beautiful working horses. Its a chance to join the mobs of people who swarm to view the cattle judging. In roped off squares, proud owners stand silently as stern-faced judges capable of

The farriers at work

making or breaking reputations move the beautifully groomed animals into a pecking order. The judge moves slowly down the line scrutinising each beast in turn, stock people give their charges one last flick of the brush, anxiously getting them into the correct stance with head erect and alert. Now the judge takes up a position in the centre of the arena whilst the hopefuls do one more circuit. The final decision is made and the winning beasts called in to stand in the order of the judge's choice. Delighted owners can now relax to smile and wave to friends as the coveted rosettes are placed on the halters of the chosen. I think back to those happy, carefree days when my own family were exhibitors of stock. In those days we were breeding and showing our pedigree dairy shorthorns, now, sadly, almost a breed of the past.

As soon as one show was over, plans were laid for the following year. Through the rigours of winter selected animals were lead, groomed and pampered, then as the balmy days of summer lengthened and autumn approached preparations became intense to bring our potential show winners to their optimum peak of perfection. A few days before the show white smocks were washed and ironed, blanco was used on the halters, all stockmen and women have their

146

The Grand Parade

own pet tricks of their trade, carefully guarded secrets passed on from father to son. The evening before the great day these favoured animals were shampood, towelled dry, bedded down in a deep straw bed and droppings forked away. On the morning of the show, to make the long hairs of their backs curl up wave-like, we used white Windsor soap, a soft soap ideal for this purpose. Tails were washed, dried and fluffed up using a dog comb.

One's pride knew no bounds if your stock was placed at the front of the line-up.

Later in the day the finest sight is still, however, the Grand Parade where a never-ending line of winning beasts circle the main ring. Proud junior Young Farmers lead each section carrying placards naming the many and various breeds, whilst over the tannoy system a knowledgeable gentleman gives a running commentary for the benefit of the uninitiated. These days you will not see dairy bulls in the Grand Parade. Generally these breeds are not so decile as the beef breeds and required two stockmen to contain each one safely.

In prominent and envied positions are the tractor and implement dealers' stands. Long established family firms like C J Day & Son, Mike Lawrence (Farm Equipment), Oakes Bros. Ltd, P.J,S. (Agricultural) Services and Walter Wilder (Agricultural) Ltd. All compete for the prizes given to the best laid out trade stands and of course the farmer's cheque book! Dawdle a while, just watching and innocently eavesdropping this can be such a treat. Small groups of

147

prosperous looking characters with rugged faces and strange shaped walking sticks cluster round giant tractors, combine harvesters, brightly painted balers or the latest corn drill, whilst smartly dressed salesmen with name tags on the lapels of their jackets, extol the labour saving advantages and improvements in design over last year's model.

Meanwhile the farmer's young son or grandson without doubt will have clambered up into the seat of the nearest tractor. In the air-conditioned safety cab, half as big as a house and sporting more dials and switches than is to be found in the cockpit of a Boeing 747 Jumbo Jet, he will be brmm brmming, turning the steering wheel, moving levers, pressing buttons and wishing the ignition key hadn't been thoughtfully removed. Breaking into the serious conversation below a small voice enquires. "You going to buy this tractor Grandad?" "No, not today" I reply, taking a quick glance upwards at the £50,000 price tag in the cab window of the giant four-wheel drive John Deere. "Good gracious me lad, I own three farms now and the whole darn shooting match didn't cost me as much as they are asking for that tractor!!"

Now that I'm taking a back seat in the day to day running of our farming enterprise and leaving high finance to my sons, I must confess that my visits to the agricultural stands are more in favour of chatting over old times and partaking of the drink and refreshments that flow so freely. I'm very partial to Peter Smith's lardy cake, gently warmed, greasy and full of currants, they make my day. One doesn't have to purchase a new tractor or a round baler to enjoy Peter and his family's hospitality, just the merest interest in a ride-on mower or a chain saw will get you a great welcome to their marquee.

A must for every show visitor is the massive flower marquee. A useful tip is to visit early in the day before this 'Garden of England' becomes too crowded. Once inside please don't rush, you have got all day, give yourself time to take it all in. In my attempt to describe the marvellous displays and arrangements I regret my vocabulary will soon run dry.

The multi-coloured chrysanthemums, dahlias, carnations, pinks, sweet peas and African violets are so magnificent as to be almost unreal, how are such blooms produced?

Banks of elegant roses, every year more beautiful with more varieties and new colours, yet still my favourite is the Queen Elizabeth. Local nurseries compete for the Gold Diploma, the Challenge Cup and lesser awards, their displays are just fantastic and great credit is due for their ability to put on such a show in often difficult growing weather.

I am always fascinated by the Bonsai trees, the mighty oak, pine, chestnut, maple and many others artificially dwarfed as ornaments, perfect miniatures of their species, growing in a true replica of their natural surroundings yet their height measured in centimetres rather than metres. The cacti collection never fails to attract, these succulent, spiny plants come in every conceivable shape, colour and form. From the tiniest speck in two inch high pots to the multi-branched giants that threaten to pierce the canvas above.

In a separate section you will discover another delight, exhibitors from surrounding villages compete in the vegetable displays. I am shamed by thoughts of my own garden produce, puny, mis-shaped specimens against such perfection. Onions, almost as big as footballs, leeks a metre tall and as thick as a farmer's wrist, carrots and parsnips straight and true, giant cauliflowers, runner beans without the hint of a curl, white skinned potatoes with pink eyes, faultless in shape and size, apples, round and firm, just waiting to be eaten. Full marks to such dedicated gardeners.

In this section is also displayed the unbelievable orginality and skill of the flower arrangement classes. There is keen rivalry in the inter-village competition. I don't envy the judge's task.

There is so much to see and do at our show that even in two full days no way can one take in more than just a sample of all there is on offer. For instance, the rural craft marquee I'm sure it gets longer and longer each year, one could quite easily spend half a day admiring such skillful handiwork and most of the finished articles are for sale, unusual items that can seldom be found in town shops.

The Food Hall. Tempting displays of appetizing goodies for show and sale at the numerous delicatessen stalls. The bakery offering mouthwatering cream cakes and real bread, not the mass produced factory variety which I call plastic bread. The almost extinct family butcher selling tender beef joints cut from a mature carcase that has been hung for the traditional two weeks. The pleasurable aroma of the cheese stand I find difficulty in passing by without tasting some of the free samples temptingly placed in little dishes, and you really must sample the excellent English made wines. Why not purchase as you wander round? One can always call back later in the day to collect before leaving for home.

Tucked away in the south-east corner of the show ground is the hurly-burly of the fun fair. The big wheel, the helter skelter, side shows and the roundabout. I promise myself that each year from now on I will have at least one ride on the gaudy painted horses as they circle the organ. As a lad I was always fascinated by this clever musical instrument and would try and figure out how the mechanism worked as I clung desperately to the gold painted, brandy-snap pole which rose from the front of the horse's saddle as my mount bobbed up and down in tune to the music.

From the air the main ring looks not unlike an emerald gem set amongst a circle of large white stones completely enclosed by the triangle of black macadam roads along which endless lines of, what look like mini-toys driven by their drivers in one mad rush to get from A to B. On the ground it is the pulsating heart of the show. This bright green, irrigated patch of grass buzzes with activity through two long days of autumn sunshine. (It seldom rains on Newbury Show day. From 9 a.m. 'til almost dark one can watch some exciting form of entertainment taking place. You can choose to stand by the rails or sit on the tiered red painted seats kindly loaned by Arena Promotions of Hermitage. If one so desires one can become a Member of the Society for a small annual sum and enjoy the pleasure and convenience of free entrance to the Grand Stand and the President's Enclosure. In the large marquee by the main ring there is a bar with drinks and food available. Between this marquee and the ring one can enjoy the garden party atmosphere of this happy, social occasion, to circulate and meet old friends, join them in a drink and watch events taking place beyond the wooden rails.

Our hard working show organisers always succeed in putting on some spectacle to enrapture the crowd. 1985, the first year on the new ground, we had the Royal Naval Display Team. Certainly an event to thrill, unfortunately it was to be the team's last public appearance. Formed in 1972 the team chose Newbury Show for its farewell performance before being disbanded due to personnel cutbacks. The team's aim was to show the Royal Navy in places it would not normally visit. The pageantry by the junior ratings involved the spectacular 'Window Ladder', where the team performed over 200 co-ordinated movements to music 40 feet above the ground without any word of command being given. They also did a mast-manning display, in which a 90 foot mast was erected in the arena and manned in traditional Navy style, with a 'Button Boy' standing on the very top.

On another occasion it was the turn of the Royal Horse Artillery with the thunder of their charging horses pulling heavy field pieces, the wooden wheels cutting up the precious turf as the teams cross in figures of eight, missing each other by a hair's breadth. Finally, the guns were fired with ear-blasting reports that can be heard for miles around.

In 1988 (or was it 1989?) the massed band of the Mounted Horse Guards in their splendid uniforms and plumed helmets put on a spectacular performance. That year my wife and I put some of the soldiers up for the night at our farmhouse which meant we got to know these lads and their horses by name with the result that after the performance at the show ground our grandchildren were given rides on the beautiful drum horse.

Throughout the day there are thrills galore to be seen in the main arena. The shepherds and their collie sheep dogs make working with sheep look so easy as they bring-in, cut-out and pen a few stubborn, footstamping ewes. Similar scenes can of course be watched on TV in the "One man and his dog" series but like being present at a football cup final, there is nothing to compare with the atmosphere of the real thing.

Massed bands of the Mounted Horse Guards

The Heavy Horse Turn-outs. Superbly restored drays and wagons circle the arena, many still in daily use delivering casks of beer and other goods. Not so many years ago the working horse almost died out in England but they have made quite a comeback thanks to dedicated enthusiasts. Shires, Percherons and Clydesdales, gentle giants resplendent with manes and tails plaited with coloured ribbons, martingales hold their proud heads in place, polished harness decked with brasswork and bells glitter in the afternoon sun. They canter round the ring making light work of pulling heavy, wooden wheeled wagons. Thundering past the crowds just a metre or two from the safety rails, stepping high, their huge feathered hooves make the very ground tremble. Meanwhile the judge in the ring is making mental notes before selecting the winners in their class. It is a surprising thought when one recalls that before the Second World War most of the land work in this country was performed by the heavy horse and the highly skilled head carter and his men. In previous centuries when these horses weren't pulling a plough they were carrying heavily armoured knights into battle on the continent. Now we send the poor creatures over to be eaten by our former enemies.

Two days is not nearly enough time to fit in everything that one would wish to see and do. For instance in Ring One top international show-jumping stars compete against each other, putting their famous mounts over stiff jumps throughout the day. Fearless children and teenagers gallop headlong in obstacle and relay races, whooping at the top of their voices to urge on their steeds to even greater efforts. Some of these young riders will be taking part in the 'Horse of the Year Show' in a few years time thats for sure.

Precisely on time, if one has very keen eyesight, can be seen a small aircraft, ten thousand feet above the earth. Tiny dots drop from an open hatch, free-fall parachutists plummet swifty earthwards, coloured smoke from canisters strapped to their ankles trace their downward plunge until at the last moment life-saving 'chutes open, arresting the pull of gravity and those thoroughly trained perfectionists bring their brightly coloured canopies under control and

Proud team of heavy horse & dray

A Yesteryear John Deere

glide unerringly to that postage stamp sized patch of grass amidst the cheering crowds.

From the grandstand on the Sunday morning, members can participate in the Harvest Thanksgiving Service. Music for the hymns is provided by the Military Band. A fitting end to the farming community's year long task of providing the nation's food. The sermon is relayed around the main arena for all to join in giving thanks to God for the blessing of our pleasant, fertile, life giving land and our hopes for the year ahead.

The grand finale, on the second day, weather permitting is the mass ascent of the Hot Air Balloons. It is truly an amazing spectacle. The main ring is a hive of activity as crew members unpack, assemble and prepare for take off. The balloons, all shapes and sizes, jostle each other like giant puppets. Then when fully inflated, they take off one after the other, filling the evening sky in the direction of the

Sunday morning service of thanksgiving

wind drift. The balloonist, pilots and a few lucky passengers wave to the crowds of onlookers below. God help them if they are forced to land on an unfriendly landowners pad!!

Time for home; why not make a day of it? Call at a local pub for a drink and an evening meal. Monday morning is still a long way off for the five day week folk and with a bit of luck someone else will have milked the farmer's cows. Most of the thousands who poured into the show earlier in the day go away with a bit of a sun tan, hopefully, a little taste of country life and a firm resolve to come again next year. You cannot beat a rustic weekend. Fresh air never killed anyone.

Guardians of the countryside

Who are those people called farmers? In the general public's eye we are those money grabbing members of society who rape the beautiful English countryside, spraying chemicals by the tankful and artificial fertilizer by the ton. The truth of the matter is we are more 'green' and 'environmentally friendly' than many townfolk believe. Most farmers respect the land, they strive to maintain fertility of the soil, doing their best to leave their farms in better heart for future generations.

Probably one of the hardest things for a farmer to realise today is that they are considered unimportant people by the majority of the community.

Some people would have you believe that all farmers are cast in the same mould and yet in my experience no two farmers are alike. Farmers differ widely from county to county. The crops they grow, the type of stock they keep, the machinery they use is in part dictated by the area in which they farm and the climate they have to contend with.

There are those farmers who were educated at private school and the best agricultural college in the country and others like myself whose only education was at the village school and are more familiar with a set of spanners than volumes of scientific literature. Some farmers dress like landed gentry and others prefer to disguise their wealth in hole-ridden sweaters and grandfather's old breeches held up with baler twine.

Like my late father, there are those farmers who buy any crossbred of livestock at their local auction, provided they look cheap, and others who travel hundreds of miles to buy pedigree stock and on arrival study not the animal but written details in the catalogue and only bid in that long forgotten coin of the realm, the guinea.

There are farms which are as tidy as their owner's minds, with acres of concrete swept daily and not an implement or tool out of its allotted place and others like ours which have lost acres of useful productive land to ramshackle, rusting machines of yesteryear, which languish forgotten in noxious weeds.

There are those farmers who drive to agricultural shows and the local point-to-point in fine Range Rovers, because they think it creates the right image and gives them credibility, and others who drive an old Jeep because it keeps their bank balance in credit. Some keep records of everything from fertilizer units applied to the lambing percentage, and others record important information on the back of an empty cigarette packet tucked behind the clock. Some can afford to buy new tractors but make do with second-hand, and some buy the biggest machine that their overdrawn overdraft will allow. Some plant hedges and dig ponds to stock with fish, and others grub out hedges and dump them in ponds.

There are hard swearing, hard drinking farmers who cannot keep their staff from sowing time to harvest, and others whose workers have become part of the scenery, only stopping work when they make that final journey to the churchyard, having collected a long-service medal on the way. Some, like myself, have travelled the world on farming tours, from New Zealand to the States, and from Canada to China only to learn that foreign agriculture has little to teach us. Others have stayed put, quite content with their small plot of U.K. soil, like a farmer friend of mine who I had chanced to take on the 45 mile journey to Chippenham livestock market. To my enquiry as to whether he had ever visited the West Country, he replied "No never been down country that far you, but I did drive to Marlborough once to fetch a spare part for my tractor. A level uninteresting journey along the A4 of almost twenty miles.

It would give me great pleasure if the public appreciated perhaps a little more the hard work we farmers do in producing wholesome food which finds its way onto supermarket shelves and the efforts we make towards creating and maintaining the green fields, dry stone walls and well trimmed hedges, which make the pleasant English countryside as we know it.

So please join me in a silent toast to farmers great and small, the custodians of the countryside.

Our Wood

Mousefield Coppice: typical of deciduous woodland on the calcareous soil of Southern England is just a tiny remnant of the vast forest that in times past covered the British Isles.

In 1750 few parts of England had been mapped in any detail. It was in 1761 that John Rocque topographer to his Majesty King George Third completed the first topographical map of the County of Berkshire of which I am fortunate to possess a copy of the original given in gratitude for services rendered to my first wife Peggy by William and Elizabeth Wallace, late of Bagnor Manor. This old ordnance survey marks 'Mousefield Farm' much as it is today. Along with every track, road, building and field, our wood is also shown.

Classified as ancient coppiced woodland it remains more or less in its virgin state. Trees die or are blown down by winter gales, natural replacements fill the gaps. Whether I am to be praised or shamed I admit that in my forty odd years as guardian I have never planted a single tree or shrub within its boundaries.

In all its moods, our wood is beautiful at any time of the year. January or February. Mornings can be glorious, a white winter wonderland with everything brushed in icy whiteness. The weak sun's rays pierce the leafless trees picking out innumerable footprints in the sparkling blanket of snow. A true record of the passing in the night of a large animal population.

March, or any other month of the year for that matter can send the most fearsome gales. I have traversed these woods with the wind so severe it is amazing that any tree be left standing. The topmost branches whipped into a frenzy dance by the violent tempest, any remaining leaves blown into the next county.

April. A lovely month, the icy weather has finally lost its grip, with summer just around the corner everything seems to wake from winter's sleep. The dawn chorus is at its best and without fail the cuckoo will announce its arrival. Yet, don't be misled, we can still get a late fall of snow!!

May. The month that my wife Ruth and I open our garden and nature trails, becoming hosts to neighbours and friends in Newbury and the surrounding area. For what unfortunately is far too short a period, our wood is transformed, carpeted from end to end a vivid blue. I know of few other woods in the area that can put on such a display.

Bluebell weekend at Mousefield has become an annual event with us. The public flock to our farm by car, bicycle, or on foot and from the vantage point of the front lawn gaze their fill on the patchwork quilt of our lovely valley. To visit the cloistered peace of these woods in which the noise and bustle of their daily town life will seem far away is a heaven-sent opportunity.

Take your time is my advice. Go slowly, one should dawdle, there is much to hear and see. The deceptive stillness conceals a multitude of life from aphids to owls. We hear the brown owls at night, their eerie call filters through the trees. They hunt their prey after dark seeking mice, voles and baby rabbits. Dead wood off fallen trees provide some of the most densely populated woodland habitats. A single dead tree may contain hundreds of animal species as well as supporting mosses, fungi and other plants. The footprints of deer in the soft earth of a shaded glade, or even the deer themselves, the recently worked sett of our large resident badger population is a sight not to be missed. The massive piles of sandy soil, dug out of the steep hillside is the tireless work of many generations of these nocturnal bear-like animals as they construct their inaccessible burrows. Now a grey squirrel leaps from branch to branch with an amazing agility, the nesting pigeons coo, repeating over and over their rhyme which sounds so much like, "My toe hurts Betty". A cock pheasant calls, keeping together his harem of small brown hens. The noisy rooks clatter in the tall oaks having dined to the full on the last of our winter store of maize silage. Numerous small birds sing their hearts out unseen amongst the dense foliage of the trees new leaf coverage. This country mixture will do our nearby town dweller more good than gallons of medicine or endless sleeping tablets. Sit quietly on some fallen log, you will see the birds gathering material for the framework of their nests, now look carefully, try and find

Mousefield fox cub

one of their finished masterpieces, but don't disturb a sitting bird they can soon desert the nest for good.

The trees themselves, of course, are most interesting, until the onset of Dutch Elm disease there was quite a stand of elm, now the oak and ash predominate. Hazel, no longer grown as a crop, was in the past widely used for wattle hurdles, thatching pegs, making walls in houses, (Wattle and Daub), also for heating bread ovens, another use on the farm was for making drains. Over the years I have cut my annual requirement of pea and bean sticks, the odd clothes prop and made the ever popular bow and arrows for visiting grandchildren. In addition, one can identify the birch, poplar, hedge maple, blackthorn, sloe, crab apple, holly and others, If you know your countryside all these trees can provide something for us, from sloe gin to crab apple jelly, oak leaf wine, holly for Christmas decorations to the traditional yule log on our great open fireplace,

We have giant oaks whose spreading branches cover enough ground to build two town houses on. Oaks that have acquired names over the years like Big Ben, Crooked Charlie and Hollow Harry. These trees would have been no more than spindley saplings when Oliver Cromwell's Army camped in the area of Ashmore Green and Clay Hill. On 26th October 1644, the day before the Second Battle of Newbury, a large force under Skippon set out for Chieveley resting overnight at North Heath before attacking the Royalist in an outflanking movement at Speen and Shaw. It is reputed that part of this army marched through our wood via the green central track, then on through the farmyard to Long Lane. If this rumour is indeed correct those war weary parliamentarian troops with battle to come on their minds would certainly not be in the mood to appreciate the beautiful autumn colours. If they did in fact march, weapons muffled for silence through the 17th Century farmyard it could not have been obstructed as it is today by a milking parlour, cow kennels, slurry lagoon, not to mention 150 dairy cows restrained by walls, feed fences, iron gates tied together with baler twine, silage clamps covered with black plastic sheets and discarded motor car tyres, tractors, farm implements old and new, broken-down vehicles and our usual complement of sticky mud.

Without a clear passage the whole course of history may have been changed by their late arrival on the battlefield!!

Diversification

Our fields shine many different shades of colour, ringed by dark green quickthorn hedges and covered by acres of spider's webs glistening silver in the golden glow. There is a certain something in the autumn sun. It is warm, mature and somehow distinguished. Filtered and refined by the seasons. It speaks of seed-time and harvests past, and whispers a promise of those to come. Yet not all harvests are good ones by any means, the weather sees to that. For decades farmers and all those who get their living from the land have had their ups and downs.

For many years after the Second World War, farmers were encouraged to be more efficient and to increase yields to the maximum. Food from our own resources was the maxim. Government subsidies were freely given. At one time there was a ploughing grant. £7.10.0d per acre was paid to farmers who ploughed and replanted old grassland. A subsidy was paid on all quality beef calves on reaching nine months of age. Prices of fat stock for slaughter were guaranteed with an open-ended subsidy to make up any shortfall in price to the producer. There were subsidies paid on the erection of new farm buildings, milking parlours and grain stores. The construction of new roads, new fences, drainage schemes and just about everything else. Governments of every colour were accused of featherbedding farmers. I didn't entirely agree with these hand-outs. It only led in the long run to the massive over-production which plagues agriculture today. However I always accepted any cheque from the Ministry of Agriculture with a "Yes, please, thank you very much" attitude. Then rushed to the bank forthwith.

During the 1980's the majority of farm subsidies had been phased out. 'Diversification' is the new word in farming circles, it crops up again and again at farming conferences, NFU meetings and in the vast amount of literature which pops through our letter boxes most mornings.

The idea is for farmers to diversify into activities other than producing food; to supplement their falling incomes from other sources, such as renting out redundant farm buildings for light industry, setting up an equestrian establishment or let off some large acreage of woodland and scrub for war game enthusiasts; to create a rough shoot or a clay pigeon stand. Five van caravan sites is another possibility or tap the growing tourist trade by giving over one's farmhouse to Bed and Breakfast guests. The nut-cracker effect of ever increasing costs and diminishing returns forced our own family to diversify. Since 1980 the agriculture contracting side of our farming activities has expanded by leaps and bounds and my wife and I have become hosts to B & B guests. Many of these are from overseas now that we are in such booklets as 'Stay on a farm in Britain', 'Go UK', 'Country Rover' and 'Pilgrim's Progress'. These excellent guides have been the means through which we have met some very interesting people. We find the majority of our guests prefer to stay in country areas where they have the opportunity to meet local people. Especially country folk who have the time to stop and talk. I myself always find time to discuss our farming life and with my local knowledge send them on the road to visit places of interest.

Over the years we have had some amusing incidents, such as the one when two Welsh farmers who telephoned one evening to enquire "Did we have two single rooms for the night?" "Yes, certainly" my wife replied. "Oh, good" came back the reply in a musical Welsh accent. "You see we have chosen a farm to stay because there is a favour we would like to ask. We will be bringing twenty sheep with us, can you accommodate them as well?" "We would require a nice clean, dry, shed for them overnight, you see we are travelling on to Guildford the next morning for a show and sale and it is important that our sheep get a good night's rest." Our Welsh friends stayed with their charges until almost midnight, combing, grooming and feeding them. Next morning we were all up long before dawn for a six o'clock breakfast.

Luckily we have stables for horses too, because on occasions we have the pleasure of putting up guests and their mounts overnight. The enterprise is called 'Bridle Rides'. Suppose you had a horse, any horse – not a specially bred beast but just a fit, ordinary animal, capable as most are, of covering twenty miles a day. With it and the help of 'Bridle Rides' you can discover the pleasure of roaming the English countryside at your own pace, in company of your own choosing, seeing everything from an unfamiliar point of view.

Mostly our guests have been excellent company and a pleasure to share our home with. However there is always the odd black sheep in the flock. We have had the few forgetful ones who leave things behind and the odd few who leave without paying, but perhaps the most hilarious were the six French dancing girls who flitted around the front lawn in their colourful pyjamas in the warm summer evenings of '89. The fact that neither our farm staff, or myself for that matter, speak French and the girls spoke no English, did little to dampen the fun!

Reminiscence on Shooting Days

Nothing gives me greater pleasure than to stroll round my farm, shotgun in the crook of my left arm and a trained gun dog obediently to heel. The opportunity to bowl over a rabbit, knock a few wood pigeons out of the sky or put to flight the rooks attacking our maize crop is one of the inexpensive pursuits of the owner-occupier. Not necessarily just for sport but to keep vermin numbers under control.

Beatrix Potter has given the general public the wrong idea. Rabbits are the farmer's number one enemy. For most of the last six hundred years these long eared, furry animals with their pretty powder puff tails have been just about the most destructive of pests, able to blight a harvest as efficiently as any disease or drought.

On my farm, Mick Lunn, a close friend, acts as part-time gamekeeper, Mick generously puts in a great deal of time rearing pheasants, keeping predators under control and organising a very successful rough shoot for six or seven guns in the season. I purchase two hundred 6 or 7 week old poults which are held in two large release pens in the depth of the wood for a month before being set free to roam the covers at will. The large acreage of maize which we grow for winter cowfeed is also attractive food for the birds. After harvest a narrow strip is left besides the covert or hard-by a hedge row and ditch along which pheasants are accustomed to wander. We also have a useful flight pond which draws a fair number of Mallard, Wigeon and occasionally a few Canada Geese. I am repeatedly reminded of a rather laughable incident that occurred some four or five years ago. The seven guns and our mixed assembly of beaters had had a hard day. We were nearing the end of the season, a cold rain before lunch had turned to sleet by afternoon and a stiff northerly blew through the leafless oaks. It was a 'cocks only' day but January cock pheasants seem to be born survivors, and our bag was mediocre.

Our small group of rather despondent guns were cold, wet and no doubt wishfully thinking of a hot bath and a gin and tonic by the log fire when one keen hunter – Roy Barlow I believe it was – suggested a 'go at the ducks'. Four or five of us agreed to tag along, the remainder made some excuse, accepted a cock pheasant from the bag and made for home.

Our flight pond is really a worked out sand pit with the water level well below the general lie of the land. There is good cover on the north side from a tall, neglected thorn hedge and scraggy oaks. To the south-west we have constructed a hide or two by using straw bales. "You'd best take the 'hot seat' Bert, its your lake and you haven't had much shooting today" someone suggested. "Well, why not?" I told myself, doesn't do to stand back all the time." Guns broke, but loaded, we all made for our respective hides. I settled down behind the straw bale cover to await the flighting birds. With darkness fast approaching the Mallards and Teal would soon arrive to circle the lake before dropping swiftly out of the evening sky to settle on the still, green water.

Now I can only repeat what I am told happened in the next hour or so. A heavy drizzle had set in, the light was poor, ideal weather for a duck shoot. Flight after flight of ducks skimmed in over my head, yet my gun remained silent, not one shot was fired. Finally, my disgruntled companions who hadn't had a bird in range all evening came round the lake to my cover quite prepared to chastise me unmercifully on my shortcoming. Apparently I was discovered in a half-sitting position, snoring gently, gun propped against the bales, out to the world, completely oblivious to the perfect targets the ducks had made of themselves. It will be a long time before I live that one down!

Walking-up grouse is inexpensive and enjoyable. I could never afford the huge sums of money demanded for the experience of shooting driven birds over the butts. Why the pursuit of this wild, 'King of gamebirds' is so enjoyable is hard to explain: walking through knee-length heather can be exhausting and by the end of a long day a gamebag will cause acute shoulder ache. The wretched flies and midges in a mild autumn will have found a persistent pleasure in buzzing and whining around your ears, and the weather on the desolate moor is unpredictable.

In the search for grouse I've journeyed to the far north-east corner of Scotland, a fourteen hundred mile round trip to the tiny village of Westerdale in the county of Caithness. It is marked on most maps of the area, despite the fact that when I was last there only four people lived in the village. The only shop closed years ago, yet it still boasts a small post office, but the elderly post mistress only sells stamps and accepts letters for the postman when he calls on his daily round. Two shooting companions and myself stayed in a tiny stone cottage. Conditions were primitive to say the least but nevertheless a very pleasant week was spent in a countryside so remote from the "boom or bust" town of Newbury that one may as well have been on another planet!

Before us was the prospect of six days of shooting on Lord Thurso's vast estate which covers many thousands of acres, this area is the largest and last truly wet-lands area of Europe and as such should be protected from the tree planters as there are plenty of other sites for forestry.

We breakfast early on porridge and strong coffee then, accompanied by Jamie the gillie and his three pointers, the four of us set off for the moors. As we stride out we are free to look over the extensive marshland, to take in the glorious panorama which extends from our feet over multi-coloured heather clad moors to the distant mountains some twenty miles away. The long legged pointers are a joy to watch as they cover both flanks to our right and left, bounding over the heather with effortless ease. Two, three hundred metres ahead, then at the slightest scent of grouse they freeze motionless, one leg off the ground, pointing unerringly with their sensitive nose directly at the unseen quarry. They seldom make a mistake.

There may be just a single ageing cockbird or there could be a covey of a couple of dozen or more. Another uncertainty; are the birds sitting tight almost under the dog's nose or up to a hundred metres ahead? When the grouse do break cover the gun must fly to the shoulder, cover a bird and be fired in a split-second, or all is lost. The flight pattern of a highland grouse differs in many ways from lowland grouse, they skim along the contours and are not usually very high off the ground. Their very lowness is deceiving until it is realised that each bird in a group is doing something different. Grouse rarely fly completely straight. If they are flapping they are rising and if gliding, falling. In both cases they will be swinging to the right or left.

Our week on the Scottish moors certainly boosted trade for the cartridge makers. We had a fair bag of birds but I was to discover that there was an awful lot of space around each target!

For the last twenty-odd years I have been a member of a shooting syndicate, what one calls a 'posh shoot' where one is expected to dress in the correct gear, barbours, breeks and hunter boots and not to turn up on the day with a gun dog unless it is top-notch. Your dog must sit motionless with the birds dropping yards away, to let it bound off to collect some other gun's bird is the ultimate sin.

In that time the shoot has moved from one estate to another nearby, some members have at last retired from the sport through age or infirmity or have passed on to the 'happy hunting grounds'. I still stagger along to take my numbered stand where the luck of the draw at the outset has positioned me. Unlike the 'rough shoot' where each gun takes their turn in beating out the covers or standing, on a driven shoot we do little walking, we are transported by four-wheeled drive vehicles across ploughed fields, over winter corn, up hill and down dale, tearing headlong through deeply rutted woodland tracks crammed into the back of Land Rovers, men, guns and dogs, packed as tight as sardines in a tin. Arriving at our destination for the first drive we de-bus taking up our position at stands clearly marked by a numbered card placed in the top of a split hazel stick. Once the guns are in line the 'boss' blows hard down the barrel of his unloaded open gun sending out a trumpet-call that can be heard a mile away. On hearing the signal the game-keeper and a dozen or so volunteer beaters plus a useful collection of well trained dogs move off to fight their way through chest high brambles, ferns and dense undergrowth or rain-drenched root crops to put high flying birds over the waiting guns.

I enjoy the social side as much as the actual shooting, the pleasant jovial company, the opportunity to get away from work for a while, even the ribbing one gets at lunch time if you've missed the highest flying cock bird of the morning.

On bad weather days I often wonder if its time I should pack this lark up. When one's toes, fingers and ears are in dire danger of getting frost bitten or the beating rain has trickled down your neck and begun to reach sensitive parts of one's anatomy, when every bird in flight seems to be avoiding you deliberately, lunch-time comes as a merciful release.

On the good days, when the birds have come over in a steady stream and one has only to swing the barrel on a pheasant and pull the trigger for success, with your neighbouring gun casting admiring glances in your direction and calling "Good shot sir". Lunch on those occasions is one of the best moments of the day.

We have come a long way since those days when we all sat on straw bales in the cramped, damp tack room, opened our lunch box and munched a couple of cheese and pickle sandwiches or nibbled at a pork pie. Now I'm pleased to say lunch is a more lavish affair. Wet clothes and muddy boots are discarded in the entrance hall then we pass through into the reception room, with its welcoming log fire and our charming hostess greets each of us in turn with a smile and enquires if we would prefer a sweet or dry sherry and politely questions what sort of a day we have had. Conversation quickly drifts away from the morning's shooting, we stand around in small groups talking over the political situation or the latest disappointing trade figures.

After having only had a light breakfast, by one o'clock, fresh air and a fair bit of exercise has left a large hole in my stomach and I'm not last through to the dining room when our host says, "Bring your glass through for later chaps, lunch is ready". What a lovely, wholesome sight greets our eyes, the beautiful polished dining table laid out with the best family silver and the whole surrounded by genuine Chippendale chairs.

The shooting lunch is the place to experience traditional British cooking at its best. There is nothing fancy, just a good pie or stew with stacks of home grown vegetables, and there is always ample for seconds if you haven't managed to get enough on your plate on the first round. Pudding follows, blackberry and apple pie, rhubard crumble or a treacle tart, with indulgent amounts of double cream, and of course, Christmas Pudding with lashings of brandy sauce on the Boxing Day shoot. Not that lunch ends there – the best of cheeses, Double Gloucester, tasty Cheddar or a Stilton will be washed down with Sloe Gin or an expensive Port. 'Aiming fluid' we call it!

Then all too soon, our host looks at his watch. We leave in five minutes chaps, mustn't keep the keeper and his lads waiting in the cold. Goodness, that hour has gone quickly, time to leave the snug warmth of the dining room and pleasant company for the rain that seems to be bouncing off the window panes outside. But never mind, I tell myself, there will only be time for two more drives before the light fails and its time for home, a cup of tea, a hot bath and a relaxing evening in front of our log fire and the television.

A Fresh Challenge

Having sadly lost my first wife the next few years were lonely and difficult, bearing in mind I still had five of my family living at home. Through a chain of events I met the lady who was to become my second wife. Ruth not only had to cope with teenage step-children but took on my late wife's home, which wasn't an easy task, plus the fact that it held many memories for me.

Giving this matter much thought, it occurred to us that a completely new home would provide us with a fresh challenge.

The stable at Red Farm was an obvious choice. It is just to the north of our market town of Newbury and is described in an old sale catalogue as "A stable for eight cart horses with accommodation in loft for hay, straw, oats and two junior carters".

Situated in a cluster of picturesque brick and tile eighteenth century buildings, it had no use in our modern farming operations. I had purchased the 107 acre holding in the early 1950's and had never made any real use of the building except for a short spell when our local baker had paid me five shillings per week to keep his pigs in warmth and shelter to be fed on stale cakes and loaves left over from his rounds.

Despite the fact that the buildings are only just over a mile from the town centre there was no electric power on the premises and until recent years no main water supply, just a deep well. Nevertheless I felt that it would be beneficial to the community if this two hundred year old, well constructed stable had a new lease of life by turning it, at my expense, into a cottage for a member of my family or better still, myself in later life.

Confident that my idea was a good one, I filled in and sent off a planning application early in 1981. To my great disappointment,

Before

planning permission for the conversion of an existing stable building to an agricultural cottage was refused by the district planners on the grounds of insufficient agricultural need and that the building was not of architectural importance to justify its conversion.

Whilst I agree one cannot have houses springing up anywhere in the countryside, I never cease to be amazed by the lack of foresight of our wonderful planners who will allow acres of lovely open green field sites to be swamped with little boxes which masquerade as houses and yet will allow a beautiful old building to fall down rather than let it be converted to a delightful country cottage.

A subsequent appeal was dismissed in 1982. On March 5th, 1983, a staunch friend of mine agreed to take up the battle on my behalf. He didn't hold out much hope of success due to the fact that the first and subsequent appeal had been turned down. He explained that it is most difficult to get planning authorities' to change their minds, thus losing face. The application would be presented in a different manner. The whole range of buildings were to be surveyed at a cost to myself of £500 and professionally photographed when light was at its best. There would be no cost to myself for my friend's

172

time except that, win or lose, I gave him my grand piano and antique playing stool!!

On 12th December, 1986 planning permission to convert the stable into an agricultural cottage was finally granted. It had taken over five years and cost a hard working farmer a great deal of unnecessary money. A battle stretching over a period as long as the Second World War!!

The first task was to clean up and clear the old implements and debris left behind by a succession of farmers over the last hundred years or so. Load after load was carted away by tractor and trailer to my friend Mr Gordon Passey, our local scrap buyer. It is surprising what money these heaps of absolute junk return.

On the south side of the stable was a lean-to in imminent danger of collapse yet stacked to the roof with paraphernalia of every description. Oak beams from previous dismantled buildings, rusty milk churns, hen coops, broken beehives, bundles of old papers, magazines and books, binder-twine, hessian sacks, plate glass, tins of tar, pig troughs even a camping trailer. A use and home was found

and after

for most of our finds. The oak beams to be used later in the reconstruction of our 'house'.

Next, Ruth and I tackled the inside of the main building, dismantling with a sledge hammer concrete block divisions. All this was removed by wheelbarrow to make good the ground that was eventually to become the courtyard. The hay loft floor, eaten away almost to dust by woodworm was sawn into small sections for firewood. In the end we had two winter's supply for our log fires.

The stable had stood unmoved on the site for some two hundred years, yet it had no real foundations. To comply with planning regulations I called in a specialist piling and underpinning contractor. Steel piles were driven five metres deep into the clay subsoil. These in turn support a nine-inch thick reinforced concrete base. At one metre spacing concrete needles protruded through the fifteen-inch thick brick walls of the building. Our old stable couldn't have been made more secure if it had been built on solid rock.

I should mention that early on in this operation the contractor's men went on strike, claiming that it was the most dangerous building that they had ever worked in and due to the vibrations caused by the piling hammer was in imminent danger of collapse. Only the erection of expensive steel shuttering persuaded the men to commence work inside again.

The small single storey cow shed attached to the eastern side Ruth and I dismantled brick by brick, each one to be cleaned, restacked and eventually used again in the rebuilding of what was to become the sitting room. Not feeling or acting at all like an O.A.P, I clambered onto the roof walking up the wooden battens to lift off the clay tiles which were then placed in a bucket to be lowered to the ground on a long rope. Ruth unhitched each full bucket sending up an empty one for the next load. Professional demolition workers would have pushed the whole lot down with a bulldozer but our laborious method resulted in 99% of the building material being recycled, but then we were not pricing our time!

Mr Les Nightingale and his very skilled, patient bricklayer Doug, who had done much repair work for me over the years, commenced knocking the place into the semblance of a house. Doorways, dormer windows, internal walls and a front porch quickly transformed the outward appearance of the building.

Realising the project would cost a considerable sum of money, I invited my friendly Bank Manager to view the site. He thought it was an exciting, worthwhile operation. Money at that time was easy to borrow, "Yes, certainly Mr Houghton, £50,000/£60,000 was available as and when required."

I had no idea how I was going to pay it back at my time of life and interest would be adding up every day too! Ha, well, the Argentine and other South American countries never pay back the millions which they have borrowed so why should Lloyds expect me to pay back my little bit of a loan!!

The relatively mild winter of 1988/89 allowed work on the conversion to make progress after all the man-made delays and setbacks of the past. I was beginning to hope that a completion date could be forecast. Unfortunately, blue skies don't last for ever. One bright winter's morning a car pulled up in the farmyard, out steps a little man with a mass of official looking papers under his arm. Introducing himself as so and so, he informs me that he is from the planning office. Reading from a long list of typewritten forms, it all boiled down to the fact that some unfriendly neighbour had made a complaint, since the conversion was classed as an agricultural cottage for a stockman, the livestock had to be on the farm before the man. In the meantime, all work on the building must cease forthwith.

Now what stupid red tape nonsense was an order like that? If I rear extra stock in the farm buildings before either myself or a workman was on the premises to look after them one couldn't give young rearing stock the individual care and attention they need, also in those isolated, unlit buildings they could be vandalised or even rustled in the night!

Assuming that to argue with authority would be pointless, Ruth and I set-to preparing buildings for weaned calves.

Two days later whilst working in the big barn, round the corner appeared two tall sombre looking men both dressed in well tailored dark check suits, looking for all the world like two characters from Hitler's Gestapo. "We are from the Council and have called to inspect buildings and confirm you are complying with regulations" states voice of authority. "You are not dressed for a farm walk, where's your wellies?" I ask, casting a glance at their highly polished black shoes.

A job well done

Leading the way across the yard to a range of buildings already filled to capacity with livestock, two very disgruntled planners follow, picking their way through ankle deep mud.

It didn't take them long to decide that they had seen enough, it was very much a farmyard. A farm cottage on the premises was essential but something told me that no way would these two men in black be applying for a job as stockmen!!

After trying unsuccessfully to wipe mud off their shoes on short winter grass, they got into their car and vanished round the corner of the farm lane. I smiled quietly to myself knowing they would never return.

In the course of time the conversion from stable to country cottage was complete. On May 9th, 1990 after forty-four years at Mousefield I took up residence. Ruth and I have every reason to be proud of our achievement.